Jan Venolia

Write Right!

A Desktop Digest of
Punctuation, Grammar, and Style

TEN SPEED PRESS

PERIWINKLE PRESS

Also written by Jan Venolia
Better Letters: A Handbook of Business and Personal Correspondence
Rewrite Right! How to Revise Your Way to Better Writing

1🕮

Ten Speed Press
P.O. Box 7123
Berkeley, California 94707

Library of Congress Catalogue Number 88-051085
ISBN 0-89815-259-3 (paperbound)
ISBN 0-89815-260-7 (spiralbound)

Cover Design by Fifth Street Design
Book Design by Nancy Austin
Illustrations by Ellen J. Sasaki
Typeset by Designer Type
Printed in the United States of America

6 7 8 9 10 — 95 94 93 92 91

*... to write and read
comes by nature.*

Shakespeare

This book is for
those who still have to
struggle a bit.

Jan Venolia

☆ SIGN ABOVE EDWIN NEWMAN'S DOOR

See Confused and Abused Words, p. 103.

Contents

Please Read This First

Our language is alive—maybe not always alive and well, but alive and kicking. Its vitality shows in its ability to change and accommodate. In the decade since *Write Right!* first appeared, our vocabularies have absorbed new words (miniseries, carryon), and old words have acquired new guises (nouns have become verbs, and vice versa). Some words have taken on new meanings, occasionally rendering them more useful, but more often losing their original nuances. Conventions of grammar and usage have been altered, abandoned, and occasionally vigorously defended.

My goal in this edition of *Write Right!* is to point to some of these changes, suggesting areas where traditional usage has value and others where relaxing the rules benefits us all. *Write Right!* originally grew from two observations I made during my years as a freelance writer and editor: Certain types of errors occur repeatedly, and improvement in those areas alone markedly improves the quality of writing. The present edition retains this emphasis while taking a look at some recent changes in the American language.

> *Language rests upon use; anything used long enough by enough people will become standard.*
> —Charlton Laird

George Orwell described language as "an instrument which we shape for our own purposes." Consider the way you use language as a vote, as your way of resisting change or demanding it—in short, of exercising some control over what becomes standard.

Write Right! guides you through the standards of good writing, making the rules accessible for everyday use. As you skim through the pages to become familiar with what is covered, note the Glossary in the back of the book; it should help you understand any unfamiliar terms. Note also that I often substitute examples for textbook-style rules in order to clarify a point. Between the examples and the Glossary, you should be able to grasp any rule that isn't immediately obvious. If you have a question that is not answered in these pages, check the books listed in the Bibliography.

Confused and Abused Words may be one of the most useful chapters in the book. It sorts out pairs of words such as *affect* and *effect, fewer* and *less;* it brings you up to date on the status of words like *enthuse* and *hopefully.* The correct choice in such matters bears directly upon the professional appearance of your writing.

If you are familiar with my books, you know that I am fond of quotations. This edition provides some new ones for those who share my enthusiasm and have asked for more. While enjoying the words of Mark Twain or George Bernard Shaw, remember that they illustrate rules or provide insights into good writing.

Good writing gives you ample room for self-expression; its rules never demand ambiguity or awkwardness as the price of communication. If you feel forced to choose between awkwardness and error, you can probably revise to avoid both.

As I reviewed the changes in our language, I was impressed that good writing today strives to make the reader's job easier, clearing away distracting clutter and obstacles. I hope you find *Write Right!* an ally in this task.

> *Writing is easy. All you have to do is cross out the wrong words.*—Mark Twain

A comma sets off introductory elements. See Rule 12 (d), p. 19.

Punctuation Pointers

Punctuation Pointers

Contemporary usage calls for just enough punctuation to keep the reader moving effortlessly through a sentence. Good punctuation tells the reader what is important, which items belong together, when to pause, and whether something is omitted. Incorrect punctuation, on the other hand, can mislead, distort meaning, and interrupt the flow of ideas.

Your choice of punctuation is usually determined by what you want to say or emphasize. If you keep in mind that your goal is to help the reader understand your meaning, many choices become automatic.

When you find a sentence particularly hard to punctuate, the problem may not be punctuation but writing style. Rewriting a basically flawed sentence may be the best alternative.

> *The workmanlike sentence almost punctuates itself.*
> —Wilson Follett

The Apostrophe

1. Use an apostrophe to indicate possession.

a) **With singular words, regardless of final consonant, and with plural words that do not end in** *s,* **add** *'s.*

writer's cramp	the witness's testimony
a dog's life	OSHA's restrictions
children's hour	the employee's paycheck

With the exception of ancient proper names, which receive the apostrophe only, this rule also applies to proper nouns.

Tom Mix's horse   Roy Harris's music
Jesus' disciples   Achilles' heel

b) **With plural words that end with *s,* add only an apostrophe.**

the Davises' vacation   the flight attendants' duties
writers' conference   employees' union
the Morrises' house   the witnesses' testimony

Psychiatry enables us to correct our faults by confessing our parents' shortcomings.
—Laurence J. Peter

Be sure you have the plural form of the word before you add the apostrophe: the Morrises' house, *not* the Morris' house or the Morris's house.

Note: The pronouns *its, hers, his, theirs, yours, ours,* and *whose* are already possessive and do not need an apostrophe to show possession.

The land is ours (not *our's*).

We have an epidemic of surplus apostrophes: Tomato's for sale, 'till, Yankee's Go Home. The mistake of adding an apostrophe to the possessive pronoun *its* is particularly common—and it broadcasts the ignorance of the writer. Remember that an apostrophe in the word *it's* indicates a contraction of *it is* or *it has*.

It's not easy to put the apostrophe in its place.

Tom and Dick's boat.

c) If possession is common to two or more individuals, add '*s* to the last name only.

> Tom and Dick's boat (*not* Tom's and Dick's boat)

But if possession is not common, make each noun possessive.

> the secretary's and the treasurer's reports

d) Treat possessives of compound words as follows:

In *singular* compound words, add '*s* to the end of the last word.

> father-in-law's will   notary public's signature

With *plural* compound words, use an *of* phrase to show possession.

> the meeting of the attorneys general
> (*not* the attorneys general's meeting)

(See Rule 50d regarding formation of plural compounds.)

Tom's and Dick's boats.

e) Use ' or 's in established idiomatic phrases even though ownership is not involved.

two dollars' worth   a month's vacation
a stone's throw   today's jittery market
five years' experience (*or* five years of experience)

Sometimes a hyphenated form is better: a two-week vacation.

f) Avoid using 's in the following cases:

With titles:

Poor: *Catcher in the Rye*'s ending
Better: the ending of *Catcher in the Rye*

With acronyms:

Poor: IRS' (or IRS's) policies
Better: IRS policies

Although the possessive 's is often correct with inanimate objects (state's rights, the law's effect), use an *of* phrase where the possessive would be awkward.

Poor: the Tower of London's interior
Better: the interior of the Tower of London

Poor: the table's foot
Better: the foot of the table

Where usage is more descriptive than possessive, omit the apostrophe.

Actors Equity   Teachers College
printers union   citizens band radio
United Nations vote   United States foreign policy

Follow established usage in proper names.

Pike's Peak, Mother's Day, Harpers Ferry

2. Use an apostrophe in contractions to indicate omission of letters or numbers.

> summer of '42, can't, won't, he's, they're
>
> *I'm not denyin' the women are foolish: God*
> *Almighty made 'em to match the men.*
> —George Eliot
>
> *He hasn't a single redeeming vice.* —Oscar Wilde
>
> *It isn't necessary to be rich and famous to be happy.*
> *It's only necessary to be rich.* —Alan Alda

Most contractions are inappropriate in formal writing, but you should use them to avoid a stilted sentence or to create a friendly tone.

Formal, somewhat stilted: We are sure that is all the time you will need.

More casual: We are sure that's all the time you will need.
> *or*
> We're sure that's all the time you will need.

If you have doubts about a contraction, mentally return it to its uncontracted form to see if the sentence makes sense.

> you're welcome (you are welcome),
> *not* your welcome

3. Use an apostrophe with nouns that are followed by a gerund (see Glossary for definition of gerund).

> The plane's leaving on time amazed us all.
>
> Six weeks in a cast was the result of Donna's skiing.

4. Use an apostrophe to form the following plurals:

a) abbreviations that have periods

   M.D.'s

b) letters where the addition of *s* alone would be confusing

   p's and q's

c) words used merely as words without regard to their meaning

   Don't give me any *if's, and's,* or *but's.*

The expression *do's and don'ts* is a special case that illustrates the need to be flexible. Add an apostrophe to the word *do* when making it plural, because *dos* without the apostrophe is confusing. Add only *s* to *don't,* because it already has one apostrophe, and two apostrophes create a strange-looking word (*don't's*).

The Colon

The colon is a mark of anticipation, as the following rules illustrate.

5. Use a colon before a list, summary, long quotation, or final clause that explains or amplifies preceding matter. Capitalize the first letter following the colon only if it begins a complete statement, a quotation, or more than one sentence. (See Rule 41.)

In two words: im possible. —Samuel Goldwyn

A wise statesman once said: The art of taxation consists in so plucking the goose as to obtain the largest amount of feathers with the least possible amount of hissing.

Marriage may be compared to a cage: The birds outside despair to get in and those within despair to get out.—Montaigne

I know only two tunes: one of them is "Yankee Doodle" and the other is not.—Ulysses S. Grant

6. Use a colon following a phrase in which the words *as follows* or *the following* are either expressed or implied.

The ingredients of a diplomat's life have been identified as follows: protocol, alcohol, and Geritol.

Many hazards await the unwary consumer: deceptive packaging, misleading labels, and shoddy workmanship.

7. Use a colon in the following situations:

a) in formal salutations

Dear Mrs. Evans:

b) in ratios

3:1

c) to indicate dialogue

Margaret Fuller: I accept the universe.
Thomas Carlyle: Gad! She'd better!

> *Note:* Do not use a colon when the items of a list come immediately after a verb or preposition.
>
> **Wrong:** The job requirements are: typing, shorthand, and bookkeeping.
>
> **Right:** The job requirements are typing, shorthand, and bookkeeping.

The Comma

When you have trouble getting the commas right, chances are you're trying to patch up a poorly structured sentence.—Claire Kehrwald Cook

8. Use a comma to separate independent clauses that are joined by such coordinating conjunctions as *and, but, or, nor, for, yet,* **and** *so.* **(An independent clause, also known as the main clause, makes a complete statement.)**

> *The optimist proclaims that we live in the best of all possible worlds, and the pessimist fears this is true.*
> —James Branch Cabell

> *I respect faith, but doubt is what gets you an education.*—Wilson Mizner

Unless a comma is required to prevent misreading, you may omit it between short, closely related clauses.

> *Keep your face to the sunshine and you cannot see the shadow.* —Helen Keller

> *We are born princes and the civilizing process turns us into frogs.* —Eric Berne

If the clauses are long and contain commas, use a semicolon rather than a comma to separate them.

> *If a man begins with certainties, he shall end in doubts; but if he will be content to begin with doubts, he shall end in certainties.* —Francis Bacon

Use a comma between dependent and main clause only when the dependent clause precedes the main clause. (Dependent clauses are incomplete statements that cannot stand alone; they are underlined in the following examples.)

> *If you can't say anything good about someone, sit right here by me.* —Alice Roosevelt Longworth

> *As scarce as truth is, the supply has always been in excess of demand.* —Josh Billings

> *By the time the youngest children have learned to keep the house tidy, the oldest grandchildren are on hand to tear it to pieces.* —Christopher Morley

9. Use commas to separate three or more items in a series.

Whether to use a final comma in a series—a, b, and c *vs.* a, b and c—has been alternately optional and required as language styles have changed. Current usage makes the final comma mandatory.

> *Writing is just having a sheet of paper, a pen, and*
> *not a shadow of an idea of what you're going to say.*
> —Françoise Sagan

> *Early to rise and early to bed*
> *Makes a man healthy, wealthy, and dead.*
> —Ogden Nash

Using the final comma gives equal weight to each item and avoids confusion. The following sentence illustrates how an omitted final comma can create ambiguity.

> The 15-member marching band, a drum major
> carrying the flag and 20 Girl Scouts were all
> part of the 4th of July parade.

The elements in the series may be short independent clauses.

> *The only way to keep your health is to eat what you*
> *don't want, drink what you don't like, and do what*
> *you'd rather not.* —Mark Twain

When the elements in the series are joined by conjunctions such as *and* or *or,* omit the commas.

> *As soon as questions of will or decision or reason or*
> *choice of action arise, human science is at a loss.*
> —Noam Chomsky

10. Use commas between consecutive adjectives that modify the same noun.

> an expensive, wasteful program

> *Conscience is a small, still voice that makes minority*
> *reports.* —Franklin P. Jones

Not all consecutive adjectives modify the same noun. In the following examples the first adjective modifies the combination created by the second adjective and the noun. In such cases, omit the comma.

average urban voter	cold roast beef
white tennis shoes	short time span

An easy way to determine if an adjective modifies only a noun instead of the combination of adjective and noun is to insert the word *and* between the two adjectives. "Expensive and wasteful" works but "white and tennis" doesn't. Use a comma only between those adjectives where *and* would be plausible.

The phrase "an ugly, old fur coat" illustrates both the use of a comma and its omission. "Ugly and old" sounds right, but "old and fur coat" doesn't; hence, only *ugly* and *old* are separated by a comma.

white tennis shoes   *ugly, old fur coat*

11. Use commas where needed for clarity.

a) to separate identical or similar words

Whatever you do, do well.

b) to provide a pause or avoid confusion

If he chooses, Williams can take over the program.

Once you understand, the reason is clear.

c) to indicate omission of a word or words

*When angry, count ten before you speak: if very
angry, a hundred.* —Thomas Jefferson

12. Use a comma to set off certain elements.

a) contrasting words or phrases

Advice is judged by results, not by intentions.
—Cicero

The fool wonders, the wise man asks.
—Benjamin Disraeli

The less you write, the better it must be.
—Jules Renard

b) phrases that are parenthetical, disruptive, or out of order

*Pessimism, when you get used to it, is just as
agreeable as optimism.* —Arnold Bennett

*Great blunders are often made, like large ropes, of a
multitude of fibers.* —Victor Hugo

Every man is, or hopes to be, an idler.
—Samuel Johnson

c) nonrestrictive elements

As their name implies, nonrestrictive elements add non-essential information and are thus appropriately separated from the sentence by commas. If the nonrestrictive element is in the middle of the sentence, be sure to enclose it in a *pair* of commas; this helps the reader bridge the gap between what comes before and after the clause.

> *Earth, the only truly closed ecosystem any of us knows about, is an organism.* —Lewis Thomas

> *Unlike Andy Rooney, who puts out a book every year, I at least have the courtesy to wait two years before I offer something new.* —Art Buchwald

> Laurence J. Peter, author of *The Peter Principle*, defined an optimist as one who believes that marriage is a gamble.

Omit the commas if the element is defining (restrictive). In the following examples, the restrictive elements are underlined; they define *which* form of taxation, *which* conservative, and *which* radical.

> *Inflation is the one form of taxation <u>that can be imposed without legislation.</u>* —Milton Friedman

> *The conservative <u>who resists change</u> is as valuable as the radical <u>who proposes it.</u>*
> —Will and Ariel Durant

d) introductory elements

> *Contrary to popular belief, English women do not wear tweed nightgowns.* —Hermione Gingold

> *In general, the art of government consists in taking as much money as possible from one class of citizens to give to the other.* —Voltaire

Commas have been omitted after introductory elements in the following examples to illustrate how much they contribute to ease of comprehension.

> Ever since John has regretted his decision.

> After eating the tigers dozed off.

> If she enjoys driving a car should be available for her use.

e) direct address

> *Reader, suppose you were an idiot. And suppose you are a member of Congress. But I repeat myself.*—Mark Twain

> *To lose one parent, Mr. Worthing, may be regarded as a misfortune; to lose both looks like carelessness.*—Oscar Wilde

f) direct quotation

> John Ciardi said, "A dollar saved is a quarter earned."

> *"Take some more tea," the March Hare said to Alice, very earnestly. "I've had nothing yet," Alice replied in an offended tone, "so I can't take more." "You mean you can't take less," said the Hatter. "It's very easy to take more than nothing."*—Lewis Carroll

(See Rule 31 regarding other punctuation of quotations.)

g) the words *for example, that is,* and *namely* and their abbreviations (*e.g., i.e., viz.*)

> Some errors in grammar and usage (for example, mistakes in agreement, misplaced modifiers, and pronoun reference) are especially common.

h) conjunctive adverbs

Put a comma after such adverbs as *however, therefore, indeed,* and *consequently* only if you wish to indicate a pause.

> Sales have dropped; furthermore, employee morale has suffered.

> Grammar books frequently do not explain rules so that they can be understood; indeed they are sometimes entirely useless!

i) informal salutations

> Dear Tom,

j) dates

Put commas both before and after the year when a date is written in month-day-year order.

> Your letter of July 4, 1776, answers all my questions.

If the date is written in day-month-year order, omit the commas.

> Your letter of 4 July 1776 answers all my questions.

Where *not* to use the comma.

• **between independent clauses unless they are joined by** *and, but, or, for, nor, yet,* **or** *so*. Joining two independent clauses without a conjunction is a *comma fault*.

Wrong: The Dow industrials hit a new high, the dollar continued to recover.

Right: The Dow industrials hit a new high, and the dollar continued to recover.

Wrong: The proposal needs rewriting, it is poorly organized.

Right: The proposal needs rewriting; it is poorly organized.

As with most rules, this one can occasionally be bent for effect.

> *We didn't lose any games last season, we just ran out of time twice.* —Vince Lombardi

- **between subject and verb**

This error frequently occurs when a comma is placed *following* the last item in a series:

Wrong: Riding motorcycles, hang-gliding, and skydiving, were the main pastimes in her short life.

or when the subject is a phrase:

Wrong: Placing a comma between subject and verb, is incorrect.

- **between modifier and the word modified, unless what intervenes is parenthetical**

Wrong: a concise, readable, report
Right: a concise, readable report
Right: a concise, though readable, report

- **between elements of a compound predicate**

Wrong: On Friday I phoned his office, and was told he was not in.
Right: On Friday I phoned his office and was told he was not in.

> *He sows hurry and reaps indigestion.*
> —Robert Louis Stevenson

- **between an independent and a dependent clause when the independent clause appears first (see Rule 8)**

> *You never realize how short a month is until you pay alimony.* —John Barrymore

> *Everything is funny as long as it is happening to someone else.* —Will Rogers

The Dash

Dashes may indicate sloppy writing.

> *Unwarranted dashes, the lazy author's when-in-doubt expedient, typify the gushy, immature, breathless style associated with adolescents' diaries.*—Claire Kehrwald Cook

One or two dashes per page may be too many. Can you substitute another punctuation mark for the dash (such as comma, colon, parenthesis, semicolon)? Reserve the dash for its legitimate use: providing a sharper break in continuity than commas or a weaker break than parentheses.

A typewritten dash consists of two hyphens with no spaces around them. If you have desktop publishing capabilities, use an em dash (—) in text where the dash is in lieu of comma or parenthesis. Use an en dash (–) to indicate inclusiveness (1930–35, pp. 15–20).

13. Use the dash for emphasis, to indicate an abrupt change, or with explanatory words or phrases.

> *Put all your eggs in one basket—and watch that basket!*—Mark Twain

> *Don't worry about avoiding temptation—as you grow older, it starts avoiding you.*
> —The Old Farmer's Almanac

Use a single dash to summarize, much as you would use a colon.

> *To live is like to love—all reason is against it, and all healthy instinct for it.*—Samuel Butler

Use a pair of dashes to enclose parenthetical elements.

> *Though motherhood is the most important of all the professions—requiring more knowledge than any other department in human affairs—there was no attention given to preparation for this office.*
> —Elizabeth Cady Stanton

The Ellipsis

Ellipses consist of three spaced periods (i.e., a space before each period and after the last).

14. Use an ellipsis to indicate an omission within a quotation.

> *We are told that talent creates its own opportunities. But ... intense desire creates not only its own opportunities, but its own talents.*—Eric Hoffer

> *The man who ... dies rich dies disgraced.*
> —Andrew Carnegie

Use the following as a guide for spacing.

• To show omission from the middle of a sentence:

middle ... middle

• To show omission of one or more sentences between sentences:

end.... Begin

• To show omission from the middle of one sentence to the beginning of another sentence:

> middle ... Begin

You may use other punctuation on either side of the ellipsis dots if it helps show what has been omitted.

> *Despite my thirty years of research into the feminine soul, I have not yet been able to answer ... the great question:... What does a woman want?*
> —Sigmund Freud

The Hyphen

15. Use a hyphen with certain prefixes and suffixes.

a) to avoid doubling or tripling a letter

pro-organized labor	anti-intellectual
shell-like	part-time

b) if the root word begins with a capital letter

un-American	non-Euclidean
pre-Christmas	post-World War II

c) in general, with the prefixes *all-*, *self-*, *ex-*, and *vice-*

all-knowing	self-made
ex-husband	vice-president
self-regulating	all-purpose

d) to avoid awkward pronunciations or ambiguity

un-ionized	anti-nuclear
co-worker	re-read

16. Use a hyphen after a series of words having a common base that is not repeated.

> first-, second-, and third-basemen
> small- and middle-sized companies

17. Use a hyphen to form certain compound words.

Compound words unite two or more words, with or without a hyphen, to convey a single idea. Generally, you should write compound words as one word (handgun, airborne, turnkey, stockbroker); however, retain the hyphen in the following cases:

a) in compound nouns, where needed for clarity or as an aid in pronunciation

right-of-way	editor-in-chief
decision-maker	president-elect
sit-in	come-on

> *Since television, the well-read are being taken over by the well-watched.* —Mortimer Adler

Omitting a needed hyphen can create confusing, and sometimes unintentionally humorous, phrases. For example, *12 hour relief* suggests that there is something called hour relief and you have 12 of them; *self storage* would be a place to store the self; *30 odd guests* might offend some of your friends.

Stopping one hyphen short of proper hyphenation is a particularly common error.

Wrong: 10-year old boy, one-to-two day delivery
Right: 10-year-old boy, one-to-two-day delivery

30 odd guests

b) in compound adjectives (unit modifiers) when they precede the word they modify

> well-to-do individual   solid-state circuit
> cost-of-living increase   matter-of-fact statement
> well-designed unit   up-to-date methods
>
> *The authors adopted an I-can-laugh-at-it-now-but-it-was-no-laughing-matter-at-the-time attitude.*
> —Theodore Bernstein

If the words that make up a compound adjective *follow* the words they modify and appear in a normal word order, they are no longer compound adjectives, and no hyphens are used.

> The unit is well designed.
>
> Their accounting methods are up to date.

Idiomatic usage retains the hyphen in certain compounds regardless of the order in which they appear in the sentence.

> Tax-exempt bonds can be purchased.

> The bonds are tax-exempt.

Note: If each of the adjectives could modify the noun without the other adjective, more than a single idea is involved (i.e., it is not a compound adjective), and a hyphen is not used.

> a happy, healthy child
> a new digital alarm clock

---

c) with improvised compounds

know-it-all	stick-in-the-mud
Johnny-came-lately	do-it-yourselfer

> *He spoke with a certain what-is-it in his voice, and I could see that if not actually disgruntled, he was far from being gruntled.* —P.G. Wodehouse

The *Style Manual* prepared by the U.S. Government Printing Office has a list of compound words that I have found helpful; it shows whether the compounds should be written as one word, two words, or hyphenated.

18. Use a hyphen in fractions and compound numbers from 21 to 99.

three-fourths	thirty-seven
one-third	forty-two

19. Use a hyphen to combine numeral-unit adjectives.

12-inch ruler   5-cent cigar
30-day month   100-year lifespan

20. Use a hyphen to combine an initial capital letter with a word.

T-shirt   X-rated
U-turn   V-neck

21. Use a hyphen to divide a word at the right-hand margin. (See Rules 55–57.)

(See Rule 42b regarding capitalization of hyphenated words.)

Note: Do not hyphenate adverbs ending in *-ly* when they are combined with an adjective or participle.

Wrong: widely-held beliefs,
        highly-developed species
Right: widely held beliefs,
        highly developed species

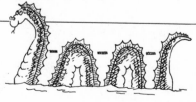

Parentheses

22. Use parentheses to set off explanatory or peripheral matter.

> *It is only in good writing that you will find how words are best used, what shades of meaning they can be made to carry, and by what devices (or lack of them) the reader is kept going smoothly or bogged down.*—Jacques Barzun

If the parenthetical matter has a close logical relationship to the rest of the sentence, use commas instead.

> *It is probably safe to say that, over a long period of time, political morality has been as high as business morality.*—Henry Steele Commager

23. Punctuate sentences with parentheses as follows:

a) When the parenthetical matter is a complete statement, enclose associated punctuation within the parentheses.

> (How I wish he would!)

> (Events later confirmed his suspicions.)

b) When a parenthetical item falls in the middle or at the end of a sentence, place the necessary punctuation *after* the closing parenthesis.

> There is only one problem (and he admits it): his chronic tardiness.

> I phoned him when I arrived (as I had promised).

Do not put a comma, semicolon, or dash before an opening parenthesis.

Wrong: I phoned him when I arrived, (as I had promised) but he was not at home.

Right: I phoned him when I arrived (as I had promised), but he was not at home.

Like dashes, parentheses can easily be overused.

> *Parentheses ... represent an unwillingness to spend time figuring out how to put things in the most logical order.... Every random thought, every tenuous analogy gets dragged in.* —Paul Robinson

The Question Mark

24. Use the following guide regarding question marks:

A question mark is used at the end of a question. That much is obvious. Whether question marks are needed at the end of every request is not always so clear. A good rule is that if the reader is expected to act instead of reply, no question mark is necessary.

> Will you please send me a one-year subscription.

But if you feel the request is too presumptuous as a statement, use a question mark.

> Will you please feed the cat while I'm away?

Quotation Marks

25. Use quotation marks for a direct quotation.

> John Kenneth Galbraith said, "Nothing is so
> admirable in politics as a short memory."

Do not use quotation marks for an indirect quotation (that is, a rearrangement or restatement).

> According to Mark Twain you should never put
> off till tomorrow what you can do the day
> after tomorrow.

When the quotation consists of several paragraphs, place a quotation mark at the beginning of each paragraph and at the end of the final paragraph.

You can also indicate a long passage of quoted material by indenting and single-spacing the text; in this case, omit quotation marks at the beginning and end of the passage.

26. Use quotation marks to enclose a word or phrase that is being defined.

> The word "ventana" is Spanish for window.

> "Qualifying small businesses" means those with
> fewer than 250 employees.

> *The two most beautiful words in the English
> language are "Check enclosed."* —Dorothy Parker

27. Use quotation marks to enclose words or phrases following such terms as *entitled, the word(s), the term, marked, designated, classified, named, endorsed* **or** *signed.*

> The check was endorsed "John Hancock."

> *I always wanted to write a book that ended with the word "mayonnaise."* —Richard Brautigan

> *A commentary on the times is that the word "honesty" is now preceded by "old-fashioned."*
> —Larry Wolters

28. Use quotation marks to indicate a misnomer or special meaning for a word.

> Some "antiques" would be more accurately described as junk.

> *You may be sure that when a man begins to call himself a "realist," he is preparing to do something he is secretly ashamed of doing.* —Sydney Harris

It is easy to overdo this usage, resulting in a cloying, affected style.

Note: Do not use quotation marks following the words *known as, called, so-called* etc. unless the expressions that follow are misnomers or slang.

> *Most of our so-called reasoning consists in finding arguments for going on believing as we already do.* —James Harvey Robinson

---

29. Use quotation marks to enclose titles of component parts of whole publications: chapters or other divisions of a book; articles in periodicals; songs; stories, essays, poems, and the like, in anthologies or similar collections.

> "Birches"
> "Punctuation Pointers"

Titles of *whole* published works such as books, periodicals, plays and reports should be underlined or italicized.

> *Write Right!*
> *Los Angeles Times*

30. Use single quotation marks to indicate a quote within a quote.

> Kin Hubbard wrote: "When a fellow says, 'It ain't the money but the principle of the thing,' it's the money."

31. Use punctuation associated with quotation marks as follows:

Place comma and final period *inside* the quotation marks; place other punctuation marks *outside* the quotation marks unless they are part of the material being quoted.

> *You've heard of the three ages of man: youth, middle age, and "You're looking wonderful!"*
> —Cardinal Spellman

> She had the audacity to say "No"!

The question, "Who ought to be boss?" is like asking, "Who ought to be the tenor in the quartet?" Obviously, the man who can sing tenor.
—Henry Ford

Have you seen "Gone with the Wind"?

When asked by an anthropologist what the Indians called America before the white man came, an Indian said simply, "Ours."—Vine Deloria, Jr.

The Semicolon

Some writers are fond of semicolons, while others discourage their use.

> *It is almost always a greater pleasure to come across a semicolon than a period.... You get a pleasant feeling of expectancy; there is more to come; read on; it will get clearer.*—George F. Will

> *Semicolons are pretentious and overactive.... Far too often, [they] are used to gloss over an imprecise thought. They place two clauses in some kind of relationship to one another, but relieve the writer of saying exactly what that relationship is.*
> —Paul Robinson

Writers today are less likely than their predecessors to use semicolons, perhaps because of uncertainty about correct usage. The following rules suggest ways in which the semicolon remains a valuable tool.

32. Use a semicolon between independent clauses that are too closely related to be written as separate sentences.

> *One friend in a lifetime is much; two are many; three are hardly possible.*—Henry Adams

> *When I was a boy I was told that anyone could become President; I'm beginning to believe it.*
> —Clarence Darrow

> *The Anglo-Saxon conscience doesn't keep you from doing what you shouldn't; it just keeps you from enjoying it.*—Salvador de Madariaga

33. Use a semicolon to separate a series of phrases that already contain commas.

The meeting was attended by Lloyd Harrison, chairman of the board; Evelyn White, chief delegate of the consumer groups; William Blake, representing the press; and Preston Tracy, speaking for the shareholders.

34. Use a semicolon between independent clauses that are long or contain commas.

Copy from one, it's plagiarism; copy from two, it's research. —Wilson Mizner

Doing business without advertising is like winking at a girl in the dark; you know what you are doing, but nobody else does. —S. Britt

35. Use a semicolon preceding explanatory phrases introduced by words such as *for example, that is,* or *namely* when you want a stronger break than a comma would provide.

Secretaries have many unpopular assignments; for example, making coffee.

Note: The conjunctive adverb *however* seems to invite punctuation errors. The difficulty lies in the assumption that *however* and a pair of commas are sufficient to glue together two independent clauses. Instead, the result is a *comma fault*. (See p. 21.) Two independent clauses joined by *however* require a complete stop (either a semicolon or a period).

Wrong: Projections were gloomy, however, sales skyrocketed.

Right: Projections were gloomy; however, sales skyrocketed.

A comma follows *however* whenever it is an interruption or suggests contrast with something preceding it—which is most of the time. But when *however* is used in the sense of "no matter how," no comma is used.

> *Let him step to the music which he hears*
> *however measured or far away.*
> —Henry David Thoreau

PROJECTIONS WERE GLOOMY
HOWEVER, SALES SKYROCKETED.

Forming plurals. See Rule 50(c), p. 51.

Mechanics

Mechanics

Abbreviations

36. In an outside address (on an envelope), use two capital letters and no period for the state abbreviation.

> California—CA (not Ca.)
> Illinois—IL
> Texas—TX

Consult a ZIP Code Directory if you don't know the correct two-letter abbreviation.

Do not abbreviate streets or states on the inside address (the address typed on the first page of a letter). This rule is often ignored, but observing it will make your letters look more elegant.

37. Social titles are usually abbreviated *(Ms., Mrs., Mr.)*. The correct (formal) plural of the abbreviation *Mr.* is *Messrs.* and of *Mrs.* is *Mmes.*

The debate over using *Ms.* instead of *Miss* or *Mrs.* has largely subsided, leaving us with a useful, marital-status-free title. *Ms.* is now acceptable in both business and social contexts; however, use *Miss* or *Mrs.* when you know an individual prefers it.

Abbreviate other titles only when you use the person's full name.

> Gen. George S. Patton
> Rev. Billy Graham
> Gov. Peter Stuyvesant

If the full name is not used, do not abbreviate the title (General Patton, *not* Gen. Patton). Similarly, a full date can be abbreviated (Dec. 7, 1941), but a partial date should be written in full (December 7, *not* Dec. 7).

38. When an abbreviated word is also a contraction, do not use an apostrophe to indicate the contraction.

> Intl., *not* Int'l. (for *International*)
> cont., *not* cont'd.

39. Use *'s* to form the plural of an abbreviation that has periods.

> Seventy-three M.D.'s attended the meeting.

40. Observe the following usages in footnotes or parenthetical matter.

Abbreviate foreign words only when they appear in footnotes or parentheses. Since many people are not familiar with the foreign words from which their abbreviations are derived, the shortened versions may be a confusing jumble of letters. They are often incorrectly punctuated as well. You avoid such problems by writing out *for example, that is,* and *namely* when they appear in text. Be sure to separate them from what follows with a comma.

Replace	with
e.g.	for example
i.e.	that is
viz.	namely

Abbreviate the word *figure* only in a caption or parenthetical reference (fig. 1).

Capitalization

Approach capitalization not as a rigid set of rules to be mastered, but as a flexible instrument of style. The primary function of capitals is to make your meaning clear; observing the following conventions will help you achieve that goal.

41. Capitalize the first word after a colon in the following cases:

a) if the material following the colon is a formal rule or a complete statement that expresses the main thought

> The company has a new policy: Every employee is given a company car.

b) if what precedes the colon is a word like *Note* or *Caution*

> Caution: Radioactive material enclosed.

42. Capitalize titles as follows:

a) In titles of books, plays, television programs, etc., capitalize the first and last words, plus all principal words.

Articles, conjunctions, and short prepositions are not capitalized unless they begin the title. Prepositions are capitalized if they consist of four or more letters or if they are connected with a preceding verb.

> Stop the World, I Want to Get Off
> Customers Held Up by Gunmen
> Situation Calls For Action
> Peace Through Negotiation

b) Capitalize both parts of a hyphenated word in a title or headline unless it is considered as one word or is a compound numeral.

> Report of the Ninety-fifth Congressional District
> Well-Known Author Dies
> Anti-inflation Measures Taken

c) Capitalize personal titles only if they precede the name and are not separated by a comma.

> Professor Reynolds
> the treasurer, Will Knott
> Sharon Weeks, president of the company
> President Baker

43. Capitalize both full and shortened names of government agencies, bureaus, departments, or services.

> California Dept. of Corporations, *or*
>   Dept. of Corporations
> U.S. Treasury Department, *or* Treasury Department
> Library of Congress
> Board of Supervisors
> Highway Commission
> Justice Department

Do not capitalize the words *government, federal, administration,* etc., except when part of the title of a specific entity.

> The U.S. Government is the largest employer in
> the nation.

> She hopes to work for the federal government.

Capitalization of departments or divisions of a company is optional.

> Claims Department, *or* claims department
> Engineering Division, *or* engineering division

44. Capitalize points of the compass and regional terms when they refer to specific sections or when they are part of a precise descriptive title

> the East   the Western Hemisphere
> Eastern Europe   Chicago's South Side

but not when merely suggesting direction or position.

central states	south of town
east coast	northern lights
southern Michigan	western Pennsylvania

Go west, young man. —John B.L. Soule

45. Capitalize abbreviations, if the words they stand for are capitalized.

M.D.   Ph.D.   M.P.   J.D.

46. Capitalize ethnic groups, factions, alliances, and political parties, but not the word *party,* itself.

He spoke for the Asian community.
The Republican party held its convention in July.
The Communist bloc vetoed the proposal.

Political groupings other than parties are usually lowercased.

> He represents the left wing of the Teamsters.

But:

> the Right, the Left

Negro and *Caucasian* are always capitalized, but *blacks, whites,* and slang words for the races are lowercased.

47. Capitalize captions and legends according to individual preference or in-house style.

The words *figure, table,* and *plate* are frequently lowercased.

Note: Do not capitalize the seasons.
Use lowercase or small caps for a.m. and p.m.

Numbers—Figures or Words?

A few conventions regarding the writing of numbers should be observed.

48. Spell out numbers in the following cases:

a) at the beginning of a sentence

> *Three hours a day will produce as much as a man ought to write.* —Anthony Trollope

b) whole numbers from one through nine and multiples such as *one hundred* **and** *three million*[1]

> *Sometimes I've believed as many as six impossible things before breakfast.* —Lewis Carroll

c) round numbers of indefinite expressions

> several thousand people
> the Roaring Twenties
> between two and three hundred employees
> in her eighties

d) fractions standing alone or followed by *of a* **or** *of an*

> one-fourth inch   two-thirds of a cup
> two one-hundredths   one-half of an apple

e) preceding a unit modifier that contains a figure

> three 8-foot planks   six ½-inch strips

49. Use figures to represent numbers in the following cases:

a) When the number itself is 10 or more

b) When numbers below 10 occur with larger numbers and refer to the same general subject

> I have ordered 9 cups of coffee, 6 cups of tea, and 15 sandwiches to be delivered in one hour.

(The number *one* in "one hour" is not related to the other numbers and thus is not written as a figure.)

[1] I have adopted here the convention widely used in business and journalism. *The Chicago Manual of Style* suggests spelling out whole numbers between one and ninety-nine.

c) when they refer to parts of a book

chapter 9	page 75
figure 5	table 1

d) when they precede units of time, measurement, or money

18 years old	2×4 inches
9 o'clock or 9:00	$4 million
$1.50	¼-inch pipe
75¢	10 yards
3 hours 30 minutes 12 seconds	

Note: Units of time, measurement, and money do not affect the rule determining use of figures when numbers appear elsewhere in a sentence (see Rule 49b). For example:

Wrong: The 3 students collected $50 apiece.
Right: The three students collected $50 apiece.

Spelling

There is no better cure for bad spelling than lots of good reading, with a mind alert to the appearance of the words. Frequent dictionary use is also essential. However, a few rules may prove helpful.

50. Form plurals as follows:

a) if the noun ends in *o*

when preceded by a vowel, **always** add *s*

studios	cameos
kangaroos	patios
rodeos	zoos

when preceded by a consonant, **usually** add *es*

potatoes	innuendoes
heroes	torpedoes

when a noun is a musical term and ends in *o*, add only *s*

solos	pianos
banjos	sextos

Exceptions: radios, mementos, zeros, avocados, plus about 40 more. If in doubt, consult your dictionary.

b) if the noun ends in *s, x, ch, sh,* or *z,* add *es*

boxes	beaches
bushes	bosses

c) if the noun ends in *y*

when preceded by a consonant, change the *y* to *i* and add *es*

company	companies
authority	authorities
category	categories
parody	parodies

when preceded by a vowel, simply add *s*

attorney	attorneys
turkey	turkeys

d) if it is a compound word

Form plurals with the principal word.

notaries public	mothers-in-law
attorneys general	major generals
deputy chiefs of staff	commanders in chief
passers-by	by-products

If the words are of equal weight, make both plural.

coats of arms	men employees
women writers	secretaries-treasurers

Nouns ending with *-ful,* add *s* to the end of the word,

cupfuls   teaspoonfuls

unless you wish to convey the use of more than one container. In that case, write as two words and make the noun plural.

cups full (separate cups)
buckets full (separate buckets)

(See Rule 1d regarding possessives of compound words.)

e) acronyms, numbers, and letters

As much as possible without creating confusion, simply add *s* to plurals.

VIPs	the three Rs
in twos and threes	the late 1960s

Use *'s* with lowercase letters or abbreviations with periods.

I.O.U.'s	x's and y's

f) foreign words

Certain words (primarily Latin in origin) form plurals according to their foreign derivation. Some of the most common are listed below, followed by examples of foreign words whose plural forms have become Anglicized. A recent edition of a good dictionary is your best guide.

Singular	Plural
alumnus (masc.)	alumni (masc. *or* masc. and fem.)
alumna (fem.)	alumnae (fem.)
axis	axes
crisis	crises
criterion	criteria
datum	data
medium	media *or* mediums
memorandum	memoranda *or* memorandums (*not* memorandas)
nucleus	nuclei
phenomenon	phenomena
stimulus	stimuli
stratum	strata

Note the singular forms of *criteria, media,* and *phenomena.* A common mistake is using the plural form when the verb requires singular (*criterion, medium, phenomenon*). *Data* is now widely treated as singular and is accepted as such by some authorities, who point to the acceptance of a comparable word, *agenda,* as singular. In formal and scientific writing, however, you should treat it as the plural word it is. Thus, data *are*, not data *is*.

Anglicized Plurals

antenna	antennas
appendix	appendixes
cactus	cactuses
formula	formulas
index	indexes (scientific, use *indices*)
prospectus	prospectuses

51. Add suffixes as follows:

Drop the silent *e* at the end of a word when adding a suffix that begins with a vowel:

age	aging	force	forcible
move	movable	route	routing
sale	salable	use	usage

Exceptions: mileage, hoeing, and words such as manageable or serviceable, where dropping the final *e* would produce a hard consonant.

Double the final consonant of the root word when all of the following conditions are met:

> suffix begins with a vowel:
> (committ*e*d, regrett*a*ble, runn*i*ng)

> root word ends in a single consonant that is preceded by a single vowel:
> swi*m* (swimming), gri*n* (grinned), fla*p* (flapper)

last syllable is accented, or the word consists of one syllable:

(remit, rip, put)

Exceptions: chagrined, transferable

The following words do *not* meet at least one of the above requirements, and thus the final consonant is not doubled:

commit   commitment
(suffix does not begin with a vowel)

appeal   appealed
(final consonant is preceded by a double vowel)

travel   traveled
(last syllable is not accented)

The following words *do* meet the requirements:

commit	committed
bag	baggage
red	reddish
occur	occurrence
refer	referred
transfer	transferred

Note: If the accent moves to the preceding syllable with the addition of a suffix, the final consonant is not doubled.

refer	reference
prefer	preference

52. Use the following guide for words ending in *-able* or *-ible*:

Any word that has an *-ation* form **always** takes the suffix *-able*.

> durable (duration)
> commendable (commendation)
> irritable (irritation)
> excitable (excitation)

Words with *-ion, -tion, -id,* or *-ive* forms **usually** take the suffix *-ible*.

> collectible (collection)
> irresistible (resistive)
> digestible (digestion)
> suggestible (suggestive)

Remember this is not completely reliable. For example, some words that do not have an *-ation* form nonetheless take *-able* (manageable, desirable, likable). A dictionary will solve the problem if you are uncertain.

> *For every credibility gap there is a gullibility gap.*
> —Richard Clopton

> *Honesty is a good thing, but it is not profitable to its possessor unless it is kept under control.*
> —Don Marquis

53. Use the following guide for words ending in *-sede, -ceed,* and *-cede*:

Only one word ends in *-sede* (supersede), and three end in *-ceed* (exceed, proceed, and succeed). All other words of this type end in *-cede* (precede, secede ...).

> *Nothing succeeds like excess.*—Oscar Wilde

54. Be careful of *ie* and *ei* words.

The grammar school jingle we all learned has so many exceptions that you should use it only when you don't have a dictionary handy. The first line of the jingle is the more useful part.

> Put *i* before *e*, except after *c*,
>
> (*i* before *e*): piece, brief, niece
> (except after *c*): receive, ceiling, deceive

This rule applies only when the words containing *ei* or *ie* are pronounced like *ee* (as in *need*). When the sound is other than *ee*, the correct spelling is usually *ei* (e.g., freight, neighbor, vein). Some exceptions are *either/neither, seize, financier,* and *weird.*

> *It is a pity that Chaucer, who had geneyus, was so unedicated. He's the wuss speller I know of.*
> —Artemus Ward

Word Division

Words that are divided at the right-hand margin are an interruption to the reader; incorrectly divided words slow the reader down even more. So divide words only when you must, and always do it correctly. Both parts of a divided word should be pronounceable, and you should avoid breaking a word so that the first fragment produces a misleading meaning (legis-lature, not leg-islature; thera-pist, not the-rapist).

55. Divide words as follows:

a) between syllables

num-ber	moun-tain
con-sum-er	vo-ca-tion
trou-sers	prod-uct
el-e-va-tor	west-ern
sher-iff	in-di-cate

Careful pronunciation will help you determine correct syllabication.

b) between double letters

quar-rel	refer-ring
com-mittee	ac-com-mo-date
op-pres-sion	flip-pant

unless the double letter comes at the end of the simple form of the word

call-ing	bless-ing
success-ful	add-ing
fluff-ier	hell-ish

c) in hyphenated words, only where the hyphen already exists

thirty-five, not thir-ty-five
sister-in-law, not sis-ter-in-law

d) at a prefix or suffix, but not within it

super-market, not su-permarket
contra-ceptive, not con-traceptive

e) to produce the most meaningful grouping

careless-ness, not care-lessness
consign-ment, not con-signment

f) after, not before, a one-letter syllable

busi-ness   poli-tics
sili-con   statu-ary

unless the one-letter syllable is part of the suffixes -*able* or *ible*

illeg-ible   mov-able
inevit-able   permiss-ible

Note: The *a* and *i* in many -*able* and -*ible* words are not one-letter syllables and should be divided as in the following examples:

ame-na-ble   pos-si-ble
ter-ri-ble   char-i-ta-ble
ca-pa-ble   swim-ma-ble

56. Do not divide the following:

a) **one-syllable words**

b) **words with fewer than six letters**

c) **one-letter syllables**

alone, not a-lone   eu-phoria, not euphori-a

d) **two-letter syllables at the end of a word**

caller, not call-er   pur-chaser, not purchas-er
walked, not walk-ed   leader, not lead-er

Another way of stating the last two rules (c & d) is that you should leave at least two letters before the hyphen and three letters after it.

e) **these suffixes**

-cial	-cion	-cious	-tious
-tial	-sion	-ceous	-geous
-sial	-tion	-gion	-gious

f) **abbreviations, contractions, or a person's name**

g) **the last word of a paragraph or last word on a page**

57. When three or more consonants come together, let pronunciation be your guide.

punc-ture	match-ing
chil-dren	birth-day

When in doubt, consult a dictionary, where you will find the words divided into syllables.

I saw a man on a horse with a wooden leg.
See Rule 61, Misplaced Modifiers, p. 75.

Grammatical Guidelines

Grammatical Guidelines

One of the best ways to get a grip on grammar is to develop an ear for the sound of properly used language. However, since many who speak on radio and television are among the worst language abusers, your best bet for exposure to the "sound" of correct grammar lies in the visual act of reading good prose. Read widely, and read the best writers. You will absorb grammar and style as if through your pores.

> *Literature is simply the appropriate use of language.* —Evelyn Waugh

Grammar helps us to introduce order into our language. Its rules communicate the logical relationship between language and reality. If you abandon that logical, orderly relationship, you diminish your ability to communicate.

> *Languages have singulars and plurals because reality comes to us that way, and we have to have some way of dealing with that fact.* —Bruce O. Boston

58. Make subject and verb agree both in person and number.

This rule seems to top everyone's list.

> *Agreement is as pleasant in prose as it is in personal relations, and no more difficult to work for.*
> —Jacques Barzun

Theodore Bernstein devotes five pages to the subject in his book, *The Careful Writer.* He claims errors in agreement are the most common mistakes writers make.

Tom is late.

On the surface, the rule seems simple: A verb must agree with its subject both in person and number. Thus, a singular subject requires a singular verb. *(Tom is late.)* A plural or compound subject requires a plural verb. *(Tom and Bill are late.)* A subject in the first person requires a verb in the first person. *(I am exasperated.)* A subject in the third person requires a verb in the third person. *(She is exasperated.)* And so on.

Tom and Bill are late.

Applying this rule can be difficult. For example, it is not always clear which word or phrase is the subject. And even if the subject is easy to identify, it may not be clear whether it is singular or plural. The most common difficulties regarding agreement of subject and verb are presented below in those two general categories: identifying the subject, and determining the number.

a) Identifying the Subject

(1) Intervening Phrases

Phrases that come between subject and verb do not affect the number of the verb.

> The *purpose* of his speeches *was* to win votes.
>
> The company's total *salaries,* exclusive of overtime, *are* $2000 per week.
>
> *One* in five public water systems *is* tainted with toxic substances.

The subjects of the above sentences are *purpose, salaries,* and *one,* respectively. By mentally leaving out the phrases that come between those subjects and their verbs, you can determine whether a singular or plural verb is required.

(2) Phrases and Clauses as Subject

When the subject of a sentence is a phrase or clause, it takes a singular verb. The subjects of the following sentences are *The best way to keep your friends* and *What this country needs.*

> *The best way to keep your friends is not to give them away.* —Wilson Mizner
>
> *What this country needs is a good 5¢ nickel.* —F.P. Adams

(3) Inverted Sentence Order

The subject usually precedes the verb. But when the subject follows the verb, it is sometimes hard to tell if the verb should be singular or plural. In the following example, the subject is *Linus Pauling,* not *Nobel Prize winners,* and a singular verb is correct.

> Leading the list of Nobel Prize winners was Linus Pauling.

In the following sentence the compound subject *a group of taxpayers and their congressman* requires a plural verb.

> Seeking to defeat the proposition were a group of taxpayers and their congressman.

First locate the subject and then you will know what the number of the verb should be.

b) Determining the Number

(1) Compound Subjects

Two subjects joined by *and* are a compound subject, and they require a plural verb.

> The title and abstract of the report are printed on the first page.

> Writing a report and filing it are difficult tasks for the new salesman.

> Motherhood and apple pie are endowed with special virtues in the U.S.

Exceptions: If the two parts of the compound subject are regarded as one unit, they take a singular verb.

> Bacon and eggs is a good way to start the day.

Compound subjects preceded by *each* or *every* are singular.

> Every man, woman, and child is given full consideration.

> Each nut and bolt is individually wrapped.

Company names, though they may combine several units or names, are considered as a single entity and thus take a singular verb.

> Jones and Associates is a management consulting firm.

> Sears, Roebuck & Co. is a major department store.

(2) Collective Nouns

Nouns such as *family, couple, group, people, majority, percent,* or *personnel* take either singular or plural verbs. If the word refers to the group as a whole or the idea of oneness predominates, use a singular verb.

> The group is meeting tonight at seven.

> The elderly couple was the last to arrive.

> *A minority may be right; a majority is always wrong.*
> —Henrik Ibsen

But if the word refers to individuals within a group, use a plural verb.

A group of 19th century paintings and statues were donated to the museum.

A couple of latecomers were escorted to their seats.

Similarly, some words take either singular or plural verbs, depending on how they are used.

Human rights is a sensitive issue. (singular)

Human rights are often ignored. (plural)

Statistics is a difficult subject. (singular)

The statistics show a decreasing birth rate. (plural)

Politics is perhaps the only profession for which no preparation is thought necessary.
—Robert Louis Stevenson

The word *number* is singular when preceded by *the* and plural when preceded by *a*.

A number of stock market indicators *were* favorable.

The number of students enrolling in college *is* decreasing.

(3) Indefinite Pronouns

The following pronouns are always singular: *another, each, every, either, neither,* and *one,* as are the compound pronouns made with *any, every, some,* and *no: anybody, anything, anyone, nobody, nothing, no one,* etc.

Neither of the tax returns *was* completed correctly.

Each of you *is* welcome.

Every dog has his day.—Cervantes

Nothing is more admirable than the fortitude with which millionaires tolerate the disadvantages of their wealth.—Rex Stout

> *Note:* When the word *each* **follows** a plural subject, it does not affect the verb, which remains plural.
>
> The voters each have their own opinion.

The following pronouns are always plural: *both, few, many, others,* and *several.*

> *Many are called, but few are chosen.*
> —Matthew 22:14

The following pronouns are either singular or plural, depending on the noun referred to: *all, none, any, some, more,* and *most.*

> The mistakes were not costly, but all were avoidable. (plural)
>
> None of the laundry was properly cleaned. (singular)
>
> Three people were in the plane, but none were hurt. (plural)
>
> None are more lonesome than long-distance runners. (plural)

The relative pronouns *who, which,* and *that* are also either singular or plural, depending on whether the words they stand for (their antecedents) are singular or plural. This is straightforward when the pronoun immediately follows its antecedent:

> The employee who is late ... (singular antecedent)
>
> The employees who are late ... (plural antecedent)
>
> *An expert is one who knows more and more about less and less.* —Nicholas Murray Butler

But if the sentence reads "An expert is one of those who ... ," which is the antecedent of *who: those* or *one?* Virtually all authorities agree that the antecedent is *those,* thus requiring a plural verb after *who.*

Wrong: She is one of those employees who is chronically late.
Right: She is one of those employees who are chronically late.

Wrong: One of the areas that has been most affected by budget cutbacks is job training.
Right: One of the areas that have been most affected by budget cutbacks is job training.

(4) Either ... or, Neither ... nor Constructions

The verb is singular when the elements that are connected by *either ... or* or *neither ... nor* are singular:

> Neither the address nor the signature was legible.

> *Neither snow, nor rain, nor heat, nor gloom of night stays these couriers from their appointed rounds.*
> —Herodotus

If the elements that are combined are plural, the verb is plural:

> Either personal checks or major credit cards are satisfactory methods of payment.

If the elements combined are both singular and plural, the number of the element immediately preceding the verb determines the number of the verb:

> Neither the twins nor their cousin is coming to the party.

> *Either war is obsolete or men are.*
> —Buckminster Fuller

(5) Expressions of Time, Money, and Quantity

If a total amount is indicated, use a singular verb:

> Ten dollars is a reasonable price.

If the reference is to individual units, use a plural verb:

> Ten dollar bills are enclosed.

(6) Fractions

The number of the noun following a fraction determines the number of the verb:

> Three-fourths of the ballots have been counted. (plural)

> Three-fourths of the money is missing. (singular)

> *Democracy is the recurrent suspicion that more than half of the people are right more than half of the time.* —E.B. White

59. Make subject and pronoun agree in number.

Just as subject and verb should agree in number, so should subject and pronoun agree.

> The Democratic party has nominated its (not *their*) candidate.

> Each employee provides his or her (not *their*) own tools.

More and more writers are looking for ways to avoid using the masculine pronouns (*he, him, his*) for both sexes. As a result, some have strayed from subject-pronoun agreement.

> Almost everyone breaks this rule, don't they?

EACH EMPLOYEE MUST PROVIDE

OWN EQUIPMENT.

They find a long history for this usage.

> *Everybody does and says what they please.*
> —Lord Byron

> *It's enough to drive anyone out of their senses.*
> —George Bernard Shaw

Often you can avoid both grammatical error and sexism by rewriting.

> It's enough to drive you out of your senses.

> The employees each provide their own tools.

60. Use parallel construction.

Parallel thoughts should be expressed in grammatically parallel terms. Thus, you can have a sequence of gerunds or infinitives, but not a gerund followed by an infinitive:

Wrong: Swimming is better exercise than to ski.
Right: Swimming is better exercise than skiing.

Wrong: The students came on foot, by car, and bicycle.
Right: The students came on foot, by car, and by bicycle.

Wrong: in spring, in summer, and fall
Right: in spring, in summer, and in fall

This principle is important in numbered lists, outlines, or headings.

Wrong:	**Right:**
1. Select the team.	1. Select the team.
2. Train the team.	2. Train the team.
3. Evaluating the team.	3. Evaluate the team.

Use parallel words, phrases, clauses, verbs, and tenses to improve the flow of ideas and heighten impact. Similarity of form helps the reader recognize similarity of content or function.

> *We think according to nature; we speak according to rules; we act according to custom.*
> —Francis Bacon

> *... government of the people, by the people, and for the people ...*—Abraham Lincoln

Parallel treatment also avoids the sexist implications of uneven handling of names.

Wrong: Mr. Swanson and Lydia
Right: George Swanson and Lydia Swanson;
George and Lydia

Wrong: Golda and Kissinger
Right: Golda Meir and Henry Kissinger;
Mrs. Meir and Mr. Kissinger

61. Avoid misplaced modifiers.

Keep related words together and in the order that conveys the intended meaning.

> We almost lost all of the crop.
> We lost almost all of the crop.

Both are correct grammatically, but only one accurately describes the situation. To avoid confusion, place adverbs directly *preceding* the word or phrase they modify.

Wrong: He told her that he wanted to marry her frequently.
Right: He frequently told her that he wanted to marry her.

Sometimes slight rewording removes the confusion.

Wrong: The seminar is designed for adolescents who have been experimenting with drugs and their parents.
Right: The seminar is designed both for adolescents who have been experimenting with drugs and for their parents.

As the following examples illustrate, misplaced modifiers can produce some charming images, but your readers may be entertained at your expense.

The sunbather watched the soaring seagull wearing a striped bikini.

The fire was extinguished before any damage was done by the Fire Department.

Be sure to purchase enough yarn to finish the sweater before you start.

62. Avoid dangling modifiers.

A dangling modifier gives the false impression that it modifies a word or group of words, but what it modifies has actually been left out of the sentence. For example:

Wrong: After writing the introduction, the rest of the report was easy.

After writing the introduction appears to modify *the rest of the report*. But obviously *the rest of the report* did not do the writing. Whoever did the writing has been omitted. Correct versions would be:

Right: After I wrote the introduction, the rest of the report was easy.

After writing the introduction, he found the rest of the report easy.

Some danglers are so subtle that they slip by established writers and their editors. Others are real howlers.

At the age of five, his father died.

Being old and dog-eared, I was able to buy the book for a dollar.

When dipped in butter, you can savor the lobster's delicious taste.

Exceptions: Certain modifying phrases have been found to be so useful that they are accepted as correct even though they "dangle." *All things considered, strictly speaking, judging by the record,* and *assuming you're right* are examples of this established idiom.

Break up noun chains. See Rule 69(b), p. 89.

Style

Style

The greatest possible merit of style is, of course, to make the words absolutely disappear into the thought. —Nathaniel Hawthorne

The following rules will help.

63. Omit unnecessary words.

This rule has long been the favorite of authors of style manuals. They often find the comparison with obesity irresistible, invoking such images as trimming the lard, empty calories for the mind, fat sentences, verbal junk food, and whittling away at the verbal waistline.

The rule against unnecessary words has taken on even greater importance with the increased use of word processors. The ease of writing with a word processor encourages verbosity. However, the technology that spreads the disease also provides a cure. Revising on a word processor to eliminate unnecessary words is a relatively simple procedure that you should exploit fully if it's available to you.

Beware of the attitude that equates impressiveness of writing with the length and number of words and with the opacity of sentences. If it's hard to understand, it must be profound, right? Wrong.

Wordy: Our proposal follows the sequential itemization of points occurring elsewhere in your RFP, wherever possible, to facilitate your review ...

Translation: We will follow your outline.

Another source of wordiness is the redundancy and sloppy usage we have built into the language over the years. *General consensus of opinion* uses four words where only one is correct; *consensus* **means** collective opinion, general agreement and accord. Thinking about the meaning of a word will help you remove some of the clutter surrounding it. *Unanimous* means having the agreement and consent of all; what is added by writing *completely unanimous?* How about the ubiquitous *free gift;* are there any other kinds? Although water heaters are supposed to heat **cold** water, the flabby phrase *hot water heater* is more often seen than the tighter, and more accurate, *water heater.*

Remove unnecessary words from expressions such as the following:

first time ever	past history
original founder	joint collaboration
regular routine	both men and women alike
unexpected surprise	ultimate outcome
sudden impulse	sum total
rarely ever	extra added features
small in size	advance warning
may possibly	temporary reprieve
present incumbent	10 a.m. Friday morning
two polar opposites	overused cliché

When you use the word "whether," omit "or not" if it is excess baggage.

Wordy: They couldn't decide whether or not to give all their money to charity.

Better: They couldn't decide whether to give all their money to charity.

In some cases "or not" is needed.

> *I figure you have the same chance of winning the lottery whether you play or not.* —Fran Lebowitz

"Rather" is redundant in a sentence with another comparative.

Wordy: It would be safer to destroy the chemicals rather than to store them.

Better: It would be safer to destroy the chemicals than to store them.

Omit unnecessary prepositions.

> all of the details = all the details
> finish up the work = finish the work

Leisurely openers like *There is, There are,* and *It is significant to note that* can usually be cut with no loss. *Both* is redundant in sentences where other words already convey "bothness."

Wordy: Both tulips as well as daffodils …
Better: Tulips as well as daffodils … *or*
Both tulips and daffodils …

Trim wordy expressions such as the following:

it is often the case that	= frequently
in the event that	= if
be of the opinion that	= believe
be in possession of	= have
owing to the fact that	= since or because
the fact that he had arrived	= his arrival
on the order of	= about

in advance of	= before
in spite of the fact that	= although
is indicative of	= indicates
had occasion to be	= was
put in an appearance	= appeared
take into consideration	= consider

The best cure for wordiness is to revise, revise, and revise again. Edit once strictly for spare words. When you think you have pruned every one (I almost wrote "pruned *out* every one"!), review your writing once more to see if you missed any.

> *He can compress the most words into the smallest idea of any man I ever met.* —Abraham Lincoln

64. Prefer the active voice.

The difference between the active and passive voice is the difference between *Karen read the report* and *The report was read by Karen.*

Active   *Passive*

The passive voice tends to use more words and often lacks the vigor of the active voice. Changing a sentence from passive to active usually improves it.

Passive: Hazardous reagents should never be poured into the sink.
Active: Never pour hazardous reagents into the sink.

Passive: The collision was witnessed by a pedestrian.
Active: A pedestrian witnessed the collision.

Reserve passive constructions for situations in which the thing acted upon is more important than the person performing the action (The meeting was cancelled), in technical material (The test apparatus was divided into two zones), or where anonymity of those performing the action is appropriate (The information was leaked to the press).

65. If appropriate, use a positive form.

Stating things positively often helps the reader get the right picture. Watch for the word *not* and see if you can restate the idea more effectively.

Negative: He often did not arrive on time.
Positive: He often arrived late.

Negative: The witness did not speak during the inquest.
Positive: The witness was silent during the inquest.

Replace:	with:
did not remember	forgot
was not present	was absent
did not pay attention to	ignored

Reserve the negative form for those instances where it produces the desired effect.

> *Of all noises, I think music is the least disagreeable.* —Samuel Johnson

> *I have always been in a condition in which I cannot not write.* —Barbara Tuchman

66. Be specific and concrete.

Bring abstract ideas down to earth with examples. Help your readers visualize what you're writing about by being specific.

Abstract: The equipment malfunctioned.
Concrete: The camera failed to expose any film.

Abstract: The new health and family programs improved employee performance.
Concrete: Absenteeism was reduced by 40% when the company built an employee gym and offered child-care services.

Wherever possible, replace abstract words with concrete ones:

Abstract:	Concrete:
vehicle	bicycle, panel truck
food	steak, papaya
color	red, puce
emotion	hatred, confusion

67. Use simple words.

Why write "facilitate his departure" when you can write "help him leave"? Avoid the four- or five-syllable word when one or two syllables convey the idea just as well.

Stilted: Per our aforementioned discussion, I am herewith enclosing a copy of ...

Simple: As promised, here is a copy of ...

> *I never write metropolis for seven cents because I can get the same price for city. I never write policeman because I can get the same money for cop.* —Mark Twain

Replace:	with:
utilize	use
ameliorate	improve
modification	change
deficiency	lack
preventative	preventive

68. Avoid vogue words.

> *Ready-made phrases are the prefabricated strips of words ... that come crowding in when you do not want to take the trouble to think through what you are saying ... They will construct your sentences for you—even think your thoughts for you, to a certain extent—and at need they will perform the important service of partially concealing your meaning even from yourself.*—George Orwell

The saturation provided by television, radio, and the various print media can turn a vogue word into an instant cliché. *Viable, bottom line, parameter, trendy,* and *paradigm* have all joined the catalog of overworked words. The best way to stifle these word fads is to shun the "in" word or phrase until it has had time to recuperate from overuse.

> *Anyone who uses the words "parameter" and "interface" should never be invited to a dinner party.*—Dick Cavett

69. Avoid jargon.

In its place, jargon is useful verbal shorthand. Its specialized vocabularies allow members of a particular professional group to communicate succinctly with other members of the group. But jargon has earned its bad reputation because it is often used simply to impress—or worse yet, to provide a smoke-screen, burying truth rather than revealing it. Technical language can hide sloppy thinking; fancy words can obscure a lack of understanding or deliberate distortion.

> *It isn't that jargon is noxious in itself, it's that, like crabgrass, the dratted stuff keeps rooting where it doesn't belong.*—Bruce O. Boston

Symptoms of everyday jargon include the following:

a) Interchangeable Parts of Speech

The ability of English to accommodate the crossover of one part of speech into another gives our language some of its liveliness. Nouns become adjectives (milk carton), verbs become nouns (on the mend), and adjectives are used as nouns (seeing red).

The word *author* illustrates the process of change. The 1969 edition of the American Heritage Dictionary finds considerable opposition to *author* as a verb among members of its Usage Panel; the 1982 edition lists it as a verb with no comment.

But too often a satisfactory alternative is ignored and the flexibility of our language is taxed beyond its limits. Careful writers will probably still refrain from using *author* as a verb, and they will certainly avoid such unnecessary shifts in parts of speech as the following.

The property was bequested to the school.

Bequeathed or *willed* would be better choices.

Occasionally changing one part of speech into another avoids an awkward construction.

> The motion was tabled.

But you can find better ways of saying:

> This model obsoletes all its predecessors.
> How will that impact our sales program?
> I'll reference that question to the legal staff.

b) Noun Chains

When nouns used as adjectives have slipped out of the writer's control, we find such impenetrable chains as the following:

> potassium permanganate-impregnated activated alumina medium

or the even more amazing:

> multimillion dollar data management peripheral equipment leasing industry.

Brevity was no doubt the motivation behind both of these monstrosities, but when it comes to a face-off between brevity and clarity, clarity should always win. Break up noun chains into manageable portions. For example:

> an activated alumina medium that has been impregnated with potassium permanganate

or better yet:

> a medium of activated alumina that has been impregnated with potassium permanganate.

c) Bastard Words

Tacking *-ize* or *-wise* on the end of a legitimate word produces such illegitimate offspring as *enrollmentwise* and *strategize*. Some *-ize* words have won respectability (*computerize, idolize,* *harmonize*); even the much maligned *finalize* has some supporters who claim that alternatives like *complete, conclude, perfect,* or *terminate* do not carry the meaning of "to put in final form."

Be skeptical of these coined words. Do they accomplish anything? Is an established alternative at hand? Although some are useful, you avoid branding yourself as a jargoneer if you can find a satisfactory synonym.

70. Vary sentence length and type.

Retain reader interest by varying sentence length and by using different types of sentences. In all contexts other than instructions, a series of short declarative sentences becomes monotonous. Give your readers relief from the subject-verb-object order of most sentences by introducing variety.

Open with a subordinate clause:

> *If any man wishes to write a clear style, let him first be clear in his thoughts.* — Johann W. von Goethe

with an infinitive:

> *To get profit without risk, experience without danger, and reward without work, is as impossible as it is to live without being born.* — A.P. Gouthey

with a participial phrase:

> *Thrusting my nose firmly between his teeth, I threw him heavily to the ground on top of me.*
> — Mark Twain

with a preposition:

> *Behind the phony tinsel of Hollywood lies the real tinsel.* — Oscar Levant

Notice the rhythm of what you have written—is it choppy, lively, flowing? Listen to the sound of the words—are there any awkward neighbors like "our products produced ..."? Use rhythm, flow, and contrast to make language and meaning harmonious. Try reading out loud what you have written; it can reveal awkward passages and show where punctuation is needed.

71. Watch out for the word *very.*

The word *very* often signals sloppy writing. Overusing it weakens rather than intensifies your meaning.

Poor: His contribution was very critical.
Better: His contribution was critical.

Absolutes such as *unique* and *final* stand by themselves; do not attempt to make them more emphatic by adding the word *very.* If *very* seems necessary to strengthen your meaning, consider whether another word that doesn't require such buttressing would be more effective.

Replace:	with:
very stubborn	obstinate, bullheaded
very weak	frail, feeble, fragile
very surprised	astonished, astounded, amazed

72. Avoid bias in language.

Many contemporary writers are aware of the benefits of aiming for bias-free language: It reduces confusion and avoids possible offense. A few guidelines can help you remove bias from your writing.

- Do not mention race, gender, age, or disability unless it is pertinent;
- Avoid stereotypes and labels that reveal a bias;
- Give parallel treatment (Mr. Waxman and Ms. Stone, not Mr. Waxman and Linda);
- Find substitutes for words that may be considered insensitive or confusing, such as masculine pronouns.

More detailed suggestions for avoiding bias can be found in two of my books, *Better Letters* and *Rewrite Right!* (see Bibliography).

Confused &
Abused Words

Advice, Advise
Affect, Effect
Allude, Refer
Allusion, Illusion
Alright
Alternate, Alternative
Ante, Anti
Bad, Badly
Bi, Semi
Can, May
Capital, Capitol
Complement, Compliment
Comprise
Contact
Continual, Continuous
Convince, Persuade
Council, Counsel, Consul
Different from, Different than
Discreet, Discrete
Disinterested, Uninterested

Ecology
Emigrate, Immigrate
Eminent, Imminent
Enthused
Farther, Further
Fewer, Less
Flammable, Inflammable
Flaunt, Flout
Hopefully
I, Me, Myself
Imply, Infer
Insure, Ensure, Assure
Irregardless
It's, Its
Lay, Lie
Lend, Loan
Like, As
Loose, Lose
Meantime, Meanwhile
People, Persons
Predominant, Predominate
Principal, Principle
Shall, Will
Stationary, Stationery
That, Which
That (adverbial)
That, Who, Whose
Was, Were
Who, Whom

Confused & Abused Words

> *For your born writer, nothing is so healing as the*
> *realization that he has come upon the right word.*
> —Catherine Drinker Bowen

The following list may help you find the right word.

Advice, Advise: The noun *advice* means suggestion or counsel; the verb *advise* means to give advice.

> I advise you not to take her advice.

Affect, Effect: Perhaps the easiest way to sort out the confusion about these two words is to remember that the most common use of *affect* is as a verb, and of *effect* is as a noun.

The verb *affect* means to influence or to produce an effect on.

> The lawyer hoped to affect the jury's decision.

A less common meaning of *affect* as a verb is to pretend, to simulate, or imitate in order to make some desired impression.

> The lawyer affected a look of disbelief when the defendant was unable to recall his whereabouts.

The noun *effect* means result or consequence.

> The lawyer's closing statement had an effect on the jury.

The verb *effect* means to bring about.

> The new manager effected many changes in personnel.

Chances are that if the sentence calls for a verb, *affect* is the word you want; if the sentence calls for a noun, *effect* is the appropriate word.

Allude, Refer: To *allude* to something is to mention it indirectly, without identifying it specifically. To *refer* is to indicate directly.

> The speaker alluded to the hazards of obesity when he referred to the chart showing life expectancy and weight.

Allusion, Illusion: *Allusion,* the noun form of the verb *allude,* means an indirect reference to something not specifically identified, while *illusion* is a mistaken perception.

Alright: Although this word will eventually follow *already, altogether,* and *almost* into respectability, today it is still considered a misspelling of *all right.*

Alternate, Alternative: *Alternate* refers to every other one, or succeeding by turns: *alternative* strictly means one of two choices, although it is increasingly used for more than two choices. The distinction between these two words has been blurred by such usage as "alternate routes" and "alternate

Alternate   *Alternative*

selections." *Success with Words* states that the use of *alternate* to mean "offering a substitute" is too well established to be considered an error, but the best usage keeps *alternative* for "substitute" and *alternate* for "succeeding by turns."

Ante, Anti: *Ante-* means before or in front of. *Anti-* means against.

> In the ante-bellum days, few Southerners were anti-slavery.

Bad, Badly: To help you tell whether to use the adjective *bad* or the adverb *badly*, substitute a synonym in a sentence that calls for one or the other.

> I feel (*bad, badly*) about the incident.

Substitute *unhappy* and *unhappily*. Which fits? Clearly, you wouldn't write "I feel unhappily ..."; just so, you shouldn't write "I feel badly about the incident."

Bi, Semi: To minimize the confusion surrounding these two prefixes, use them as follows:

> semiweekly = twice each week
> biweekly = every two weeks
> semimonthly = twice each month
> bimonthly = every two months
> semiannual = twice each year
> biennial = every two years

Can, May: The rule that distinguishes between *can* (the ability or power to do something) and *may* (permission to do it) is weakening. The Harper Dictionary of Contemporary Usage considers this "rather a pity, for the distinction is a nice one—and not really very hard to remember." Formal usage still requires the distinction, despite the prevalence of *can* for *may* in speech.

capital C
(upper case)

capitol
(building)

capital
(money)

See page 99.

Capital, Capitol: *Capital* refers to wealth, the city that is the seat of government, or an upper case letter. *Capitol* is the building in which state or federal officials congregate. The *Capitol*, when referring to the home of the U.S. Congress, is always capitalized.

> People who work in the Capitol disburse a great deal of the taxpayer's capital.

Complement, Compliment: *Complement* is both a verb and a noun, meaning to complete a whole or satisfy a need. *Compliment* means praise and also functions as both verb and noun.

> His efforts complemented those of the rest of the team. (verb)
>
> A complement of 12 soldiers performed the assignment. (noun)
>
> She complimented him on the apple pie he had baked. (verb)
>
> Her compliment was sincere. (noun)
>
> *Nowadays we are all of us so hard up that the only pleasant things to pay are compliments.*
> —Oscar Wilde

Comprise: One of our most abused words, *comprise* means to include or be made up of; it is frequently confused with *compose* or incorrectly used as a synonym for *constitute*. The whole comprises the parts; the parts constitute the whole.

Wrong: High tech comprises only six percent of GNP.
Right: High tech constitutes only six percent of GNP.
Right: The company comprises three divisions.

Contact: Widely accepted as a noun that has successfully made the transition into a verb, *contact* is nonetheless an overworked word. Avoid using it when a satisfactory synonym is available, such as *phone, write,* or *reach.*

Continual, Continuous: Although dictionaries now list these words as synonymous, maintaining the distinction between them helps preserve the richness of our vocabulary. *Continual* means over and over again; *continuous* means uninterrupted or unbroken.

> Since he coughed continually, the doctor kept him under continuous observation.

> *A man's memory may almost become the art of continually varying and misrepresenting his past, according to his interests in the present.*
> —George Santayana

Convince, Persuade: These words are synonyms, according to the *American Heritage Dictionary;* however, the correct choice to precede an infinitive is *persuade.*

> She persuaded me to attend the meeting.

> He convinced me of his innocence.

Council, Counsel, Consul: *Council,* always a noun, refers to an assemblage of persons or a committee. *Counsel* has both verb and noun forms, meaning to advise, the advice itself, or an attorney.

> Counsel for the defense counseled the defense not to speak to the council members; the council resented his counsel.

Consul is a person in the foreign service of a country.

Different from, Different than: *Different from* is preferred when it is followed by a noun or short phrase.

> His writing style is different from mine.

Different than is acceptable when its use avoids wordiness or when *different* is followed by a clause.

> Today the concept of women's rights is different than it was at the turn of the century.

Discreet, Discrete: *Discreet* is used to describe behavior that is prudent or respectful of propriety. *Discrete* frequently has a scientific connotation and means separate, distinct, or individual.

> He made discreet inquiries into her whereabouts.

> The smooth surface of water seems to contradict the discrete nature of its molecules.

Disinterested, Uninterested: Cautious writers still observe the distinction between *disinterested,* which conveys objectivity or neutrality, and *uninterested,* which means indifferent or lacking interest.

Ecology: The study of the relationship between organisms and their environment. Often misused as a synonym for *environment.*

Emigrate, Immigrate: To *emigrate* is to leave one's country permanently, thus one emigrates *from* a country. To *immigrate* is to move to a new country permanently, thus one immigrates *to* a country.

Eminent, Imminent: *Eminent* means well known or distinguished, while *imminent* means about to happen.

> The arrival of the eminent statesman was imminent.

Enthused: A "back-formation" from the word *enthusiasm* (as *donate* was derived from *donation*), *enthused* may never achieve acceptability in formal writing. Careful writers use *enthusiastic*.

Farther, Further: Traditional American usage calls for *farther* when physical distance is involved (We walked farther than we had intended) and in a figurative sense (The dispute is taking us farther apart); however, *further* is increasingly used in the figurative sense (The dollar goes further in Mexico). *Further* is also used in the sense of "more" or "additional" (further deliberation, a further point).

Fewer, Less: *Less* is used for quantity or bulk, *fewer* for units.

Fewer calories, less fat.

Less takes a singular noun and *fewer* a plural one, except where the plural is regarded as a single entity (I have less than ten dollars in my account).

Flammable, Inflammable: Both mean capable of burning; because of the danger that *inflammable* will be mistaken for "not flammable," use *flammable* to mean combustible and *nonflammable* for its antonym. *Inflammable* is still used in its figurative sense to describe persons and situations.

Flaunt, Flout: A common error is to use *flaunt*, which means to show off, for *flout*, which means to show contempt. Although sometimes widespread errors evolve into acceptability, confusing these two words is simply an error.

Hopefully: The word means full of hope (He uttered his prayer hopefully and fervently.) The more common usage today is in place of "I hope." (Hopefully, I will receive an answer today.) A great deal of ink has been spent trying to forestall acceptance of *hopefully* in the latter sense.

But Thomas Middleton's view is that "... while there may be some point in fighting against overwhelming odds, trying to whistle a typhoon to a standstill is a waste of time and energy." Just as *happily, presumably,* and *luckily* have achieved acceptance as standard usage, *hopefully* will someday cease to grate on the nerves of traditionalists. For now, a strong case can be made for avoiding the word simply because it is overworked.

I, Me, Myself: *I* is the subjective case and thus should be used when it is the subject of the sentence (the *who* or *what* that the rest of the sentence is about):

> My brother and I went to the ballgame.

Me is the objective case and should be used when it is the object of the action or thought conveyed by the verb of the sentence, or is the object of a preposition:

> Between you and me, I hate Sunday afternoon football games.

> Stan invited Mark and me to a beach party.

In a sentence like the last, if you remove "Mark and," it quickly becomes obvious that *me* is the correct pronoun.

Myself is used for emphasis:

> I'd rather do it myself.

or as a reflexive pronoun (i.e., turning the action back on the grammatical subject):

> I was able to feed myself when I was very young.

Do not use *myself* as a substitute for *I* or *me*.

Wrong: The gift was presented to both my brother and myself.

Right: The gift was presented to both my brother and me.

Wrong: My partner and myself have entered into a new agreement.

Right: My partner and I have entered into a new agreement.

Imply, Infer: To *imply* is to suggest directly or insinuate; to *infer* is to draw a conclusion or deduce.

Insure, Ensure, Assure: All three words mean to make secure or certain.

> Victory is assured (or ensured or insured).

Assure has the meaning of setting someone's mind at rest. Both *ensure* and *insure* mean to make secure from harm. Only *insure* should be used regarding guaranteeing of life or property against risk.

Irregardless: A redundancy. Use *regardless*.

It's, Its: *It's* is the contraction of *it is* or *it has. Its* is a possessive pronoun. See p. 8.

Lay, Lie: *Lay* is a transitive verb (i.e., it takes an object) meaning to place or put down.

> Lay the package on the table.
> (*Package* is the object of the verb *lay.*)

Lie is an intransitive verb (i.e., it does not take an object) meaning to recline.

> Lie on your exercise mat.

Lend, Loan: Usage experts formerly accepted *loan* only as a noun.

> I received a $1,000 loan.

But today acceptance of *loan* as a verb appears to be widespread.

> She loaned the museum three paintings.

Many writers, myself included, still consider that *lend* is the preferred verb.

> Lend me your pen.

Like, As: *Like* is correct when it functions as a preposition.

> She writes like Hemingway.

> *Childbirth is like trying to push a grand piano through a transom.* —Alice Roosevelt Longworth

In its formal contexts, do not use *like* as a conjunction; substitute *as* or *as if.*

> Residents of the model village live as the villagers did two hundred years ago.

> The shareholders were acting as if they were going to take over the company.

In journalism and informal writing, *like* is often used as a conjunction.

> Sales aren't growing like they were a decade ago.

Loose, Lose: *Loose* is an adjective meaning unrestrained or not fastened. *Lose* is a verb; it is the antonym of the words *win* and *find*.

Meantime, Meanwhile: *Meantime* is usually a noun describing the interval between events; *meanwhile* is an adverb meaning during or in the intervening time.

> In the meantime, back at the ranch ...
> Meanwhile, back at the ranch ...

In the meantime and *meanwhile* can usually be interchanged. But do not write *in the meanwhile*.

People, Persons: In general, use *people* for larger groups, *persons,* for an exact or small number.

> Eight persons are being held as hostages.

> *The persons hardest to convince they're at the retirement age are children at bedtime.*
> —Shannon Fife

> *The trouble with people is not that they don't know but that they know so much that ain't so.*
> —Josh Billings

If *persons* sounds affected, try using a more specific noun, such as *commuters, residents,* or *visitors.*

Predominant, Predominate: *Predominant* is an adjective meaning most common, or having the greatest influence or force. *Predominate* is a verb meaning to have the greatest influence, to prevail.

> The predominant theme of the event was patriotism.

> The patriotic theme of the event predominated over all others.

There is no such word as *predominately*.

Principal, Principle: *Principal* functions as both noun and adjective. The noun refers to the head of a school or firm, or to capital which earns interest; the adjective means chief or main. *Principle* is a noun meaning rule or standard.

> The principal's principal principle was *Do Your Homework*.

Shall, Will: This is one instance where fading of an old grammatical distinction has left us none the poorer. Don't worry about rules regarding *shall* and *will*—just let your ear be your guide.

Stationary, Stationery: *Stationary* means fixed in one place, not moving. *Stationery* is writing paper and envelopes. A good mnemonic is that station*e*ry is what you need to write l*e*tters.

That, Which: Generally, use *that* to introduce restrictive, or defining, clauses and *which* to introduce nonrestrictive clauses. (See Glossary.)

Restrictive: The pencil that needs sharpening is on my desk.
Nonrestrictive: The pencil, which needs sharpening, is on my desk.

In the following example, *which* might refer to the word *taxes* or to the entire preceding phrase.

> Any attempts to increase taxes, which would harm the recovery ...

Rewrite to avoid such ambiguity.

> Any attempts to increase taxes that would harm
> the recovery ...

or

> Since any attempts to increase taxes would harm
> the recovery ...

Your "ear" can help you choose between these two words. Whenever you write *which*, try substituting *that*. If it fits, *that* is probably the better choice.

> *Beware of all enterprises that require new clothes.*
> —Henry David Thoreau

That (adverbial): In the sense of "to that degree or amount," *that* is standard usage (I won't buy a car that old). But "I am not that hungry" is considered informal usage, unless it is preceded by something like "John ate 12 pancakes." If readers have nothing to refer to, they are left wondering how hungry "that hungry" is.

That, Who, Whose: The rule requiring the use of *that* when referring to things and *who* when referring to persons has been relaxed. Now you may choose whichever word seems more natural when referring to either persons or things.

> The most impartial judge that could be found ...

> Anyone who can answer my question ...

> That building, whose architect is a local resident ...

> *The fellow that owns his own home is always just*
> *coming out of a hardware store.* —Kin Hubbard

Was, Were: When expressing a wish or a condition contrary to fact, and following the words *as if* and *as though*, use *were:*

> The silence made it seem as if he were speaking to an empty room.

> *If it were not for the presents, an elopement would be preferable.*—George Ade

In expressing a past condition not contrary to fact, use *was:*

> If Deborah was guilty, she did not show it.

Who, Whom: A number of authorities have abandoned the use of *whom* everywhere except following a preposition (To whom is it addressed?). Others point out that *whom*'s doom has been forecast for more than a century. It's still a good idea to know correct usage for those formal situations calling for *whom*. If nothing else, knowing when to use *whom* will avoid such "hypercorrections" as "Whom do you think you are?"

The best guide for deciding whether to use *who* or *whom* is to substitute a personal pronoun; if *he, she,* or *they* would fit, use *who* (nominative case); if *him, her,* or *them* would fit, use *whom* (objective case).

> To whom shall I report?
> (to *him, her,* or *them*)

> *Never argue with people who buy ink by the gallon.*—Tommy Lasorda
> (*they* buy ink . . .)

> *For prying into any human affairs, none are equal to those whom it does not concern.*—Victor Hugo
> (it does not concern *them*)

> *He is one of those wise philanthropists who, in a time of famine, would vote for nothing but a supply of toothpicks.*—Douglas Jerrold
> (*he* would vote)

This is the man who you thought committed the crime. (you thought *he* committed the crime) (Note: You could also omit *who* in the above sentence.)

He looks like a female llama who has just been startled in her bath.
—Winston Churchill (on Charles DeGaulle)
(*she* has just been startled)

Who the hell am I to be telling whomever whom to vote for?—George C. Scott
(*I* am telling *them* to vote for *them*)

Appendix

Venolia's Reverse Rules for Writers

Sometimes a tongue-in-cheek approach is effective in fixing a subject in our minds. In that spirit, I present the following summary of the subjects covered in *Write Right!*—plus a few not mentioned.

1. Put the apostrophe where its needed.

2. Never let a colon separate: the main parts of the sentence.

3. Avoid overuse, of commas.

4. Reserve the dash—which is—often—overused— for emphasis.

5. Avoid un-necessary hyphens; divide words only between syllables.

6. Use a semicolon where needed, use it properly; and never where not called for.

7. Avoid run-on sentences they seem to go on forever.

8. In general, don't abbrev.

9. Have a good reason for Capitalizing a word.

10. In formal writing, don't use contractions.

11. Consult a dictionery for correct spelling.

12. Observe the rule that verbs has to agree with their subjects.

13. Make each subject and pronoun agree in their number, too.

14. Use parallel construction in writing sentences, forming paragraphs, and to emphasize a point.

15. After studying these rules, dangling modifiers will be easy to correct.

16. Omit unnecessary, excess words that aren't needed.

17. Generally, writing should be in the active voice.

18. Don't use trendy words whose parameters are not viable.

19. Avoid verbing a noun.

20. The careful writer avoids bias in his words.

21. Watch out for irregular verbs that have crope into your language.

22. Eschew archaic words.

23. Proof carefully in case you any words out.

Glossary

Active Voice: The form of the verb used when the subject performs the action. See Rule 64, p. 83.

Adjective: Modifies (describes or limits) a noun or pronoun. It may be a single word, phrase, or clause. See Parts of Speech.

> *A good politician is quite as unthinkable as an honest burglar.*—H.L. Mencken

Adverb: Modifies a verb, an adjective or another adverb. May be a single word, phrase, or clause. See Parts of Speech.

> *The secret of dealing successfully with a child is not to be its parent.*—Mell Lazarus

A *conjunctive adverb* connects clauses or sentences. See Conjunction.

> *I tape, therefore I am.*—Studs Terkel

Antecedent: The word, phrase, or clause referred to by a pronoun.

> *Everyone has talent. What is rare is the courage to follow the talent to the dark place where it leads.*
> —Erica Jong

Antonym: A word having a meaning opposite to that of another word.

> spicy/bland   ill/healthy

Appositive: A word, phrase, or clause placed near a noun to explain it and having the same grammatical relation to the rest of the sentence as the word it describes.

> My son, *the doctor,* sends me a card every Mother's Day.

Article: The words *a, an,* and *the.*

Case: The means by which the relationship of a noun or pronoun to the rest of the sentence is shown. There are three cases: nominative (also known as subjective), objective, and possessive.

Nominative: the case of the subject of the verb.
> *We* entered the room.

Objective: the case of the object of a verb or preposition.
> He threw the *ball* to *me.*
> (*Ball* is the object of the verb *threw;*
> *me* is the object of the preposition *to.*)

Possessive: the case that shows ownership.
> Here is *your* answer.
> Take away the *dog's* bone.

Clause: A group of words that contains a subject and verb.

Coordinate clauses have the same rank and are connected by a coordinating conjunction.

> The wise make proverbs and fools repeat them.
> —Isaac D'Israeli

Dependent clauses (also known as subordinate) do not express a complete thought when standing alone.

> If you have a weak candidate and a weak platform, wrap yourself in the American flag and talk about the Constitution.—Matthew S. Quay

Independent clauses (also called principal or main) are those which would make sense by themselves.

> *Old age isn't so bad when you consider the alternative.* —Maurice Chevalier

Nonrestrictive clauses could be omitted without changing the meaning; they are surrounded by commas.

> *Practical men, who believe themselves to be quite exempt from any intellectual influences, are usually the slaves of some defunct economist.*
> —John Maynard Keynes

Restrictive clauses are essential to the meaning (i.e., could not be left out without changing the meaning of the sentence.)

> *The man who walks alone is soon trailed by the F.B.I.* —Wright Morris

Comma Fault: The error in which a comma is used as the sole connection between two independent clauses.

Wrong: The company picnic is an annual event, this year it will be held at Disneyland.

The above sentence would be correct if a conjunction such as *and* were added or the comma replaced with a semicolon or period.

Complement: A word or phrase that completes the meaning of the verb.

> *Great artists need great clients.* —I.M. Pei
>
> *I owe the public nothing.* —J.P. Morgan
>
> *Information is the currency of democracy.*
> —Ralph Nader

Compound: Consisting of two or more elements.

A *compound adjective*, also known as a unit modifier, consists of two or more adjectives modifying the same noun.

> *That swarming, million-footed, tower-masted, and sky-soaring citadel that bears the name of the Island of Manhattan.* —Thomas Wolfe

A *compound sentence* consists of two or more independent clauses.

> *A little learning is a dangerous thing, but a lot of ignorance is just as bad.* —Bob Edwards

A *compound subject* consists of two or more subjects having the same verb.

> *Papa, potatoes, poultry, prunes, and prism are all very good words for the lips: especially prunes and prism.* —Charles Dickens

A *compound verb* consists of two or more verbs having the same subject.

> *Democracy is the theory that the common people know what they want and deserve to get it good and hard.* —H.L. Mencken

Conjunction: A single word or group of words that connects other words or groups of words. See Parts of Speech and Adverb, Conjunctive.

Coordinate conjunctions connect words, phrases, or clauses of equal rank; for example, *and, but, or, nor, for, however, moreover, then, therefore, yet, still, both/and, not only/but also, either/or, neither/nor.*

Subordinate conjunctions connect clauses of unequal rank (i.e., an independent and a dependent clause). Examples are *as, as if, because, if, since, that, till, unless, when, where, whether.*

Dangling Modifier: A modifier with an unclear reference. See p. 76.

Gerund: The *-ing* form of a verb that serves as a noun.
> *Seeing* is *believing.*
> Does anyone object to my *smoking?*

(Note the possessive pronoun; "Does anyone object to *me* smoking?" would be incorrect.)

Idiom: Idiomatic expressions, such as *rubbing someone the wrong way,* do not conform to the logic of a language. Either the meaning of the expression cannot be derived from the meaning of the individual words (*to take in, to make up for*), or their construction violates grammatical rules (*Take it easy,* not *Take it easily*).

Infinitive: The form of a verb used with *to.*
> *I don't want to achieve immortality through my work. I want to achieve it through not dying.*
> —Woody Allen

Split infinitives (words inserted between *to* and the verb) have long been an acceptable way to avoid awkward writing.
> Feel free *to utterly disregard* this rule!

Misplaced Modifier: A modifier that gives a misleading meaning by being incorrectly placed in a sentence. See p. 75.

Nonrestrictive Elements: Words, phrases, or clauses that are not essential to the meaning.

Noun: A word that names a person, place, thing, quality or act. See Parts of Speech.

A *proper noun* names a specific person, place, or thing; it is capitalized.
> the Big Apple, Julius Caesar, Hallowe'en

Number: Changes made, such as adding an *s*, to reflect whether a word is singular or plural.

> **Singular:** a porcupine
> **Plural:** three porcupines

Object: The word or phrase that names the thing acted upon by the subject and verb. Objects are complements; they complete the meaning of the verb.

> She visited *the ancient cathedral.*

A *direct object* names the thing acted upon by the subject.

> I bought a *book.*

An *indirect object* receives whatever is named by the direct object.

> I bought *Aunt Hester* a book.

You can identify the direct object by following the subject and verb with the question "What?" I bought what? A book. You can identify the indirect object by asking *who* received whatever is named by the direct object. Who received the book? Aunt Hester.

Participle: A form of a verb that has some of the properties of an adjective and some of a verb. Like an adjective, it can modify a noun or pronoun; like a verb, it can take an object.

> *Success is getting what you want; happiness is wanting what you get.* —Charles F. Kettering

Glowing coals, *grayed* collars, *run-down* heels, and *whipped* cream are examples of verb forms that function as adjectives, and thus are participles.

Parts of Speech: Nouns, pronouns, verbs, adjectives, adverbs, prepositions, conjunctions, and interjections. In the days of *McGuffey's Reader,* students used to learn the parts of speech with the help of the following jingle:

> A NOUN's the name of anything,
> As, *school* or *garden, hoop* or *swing.*
>
> ADJECTIVES tell the kind of noun;
> As, *great, small, pretty, white,* or *brown.*
>
> Instead of nouns the PRONOUNS stand:
> *Their* heads, *your* face, *its* paw, *his* hand.
>
> VERBS tell of something being done:
> You *read, count, sing, laugh, jump,* or *run.*
>
> How things are done the ADVERBS tell;
> As, *slowly, quickly, ill,* or *well.*
>
> CONJUNCTIONS join the words together;
> As, men *and* women, wind *or* weather.
>
> The PREPOSITION stands before
> a noun; as, *in* or *through* a door.
>
> The INTERJECTION shows surprise;
> As, *Oh!* how pretty! *Ah!* how wise!

Passive Voice: The form of the verb used when the subject is the receiver of the action. See Rule 64, p. 83.

Person: Person denotes the speaker (first person), the person spoken to (second person), or the person or thing spoken of (third person).

Possessive: Showing ownership; also known as the genitive case. See Case.

> *He is a sheep in sheep's clothing.*
> —Winston Churchill

Predicate: A group of words that makes a statement or asks a question about the subject of a sentence. A *simple predicate* consists of a verb (*can preach,* in the following example). A *complete predicate* includes verbs, modifiers, objects, and complements (*can preach a better sermon with your life than with your lips*).

> *You can preach a better sermon with your life than with your lips.*—Oliver Goldsmith

Prefix: A word element that is attached to the front of a root word and changes the meaning of the root: *dis*belief, *in*attentive.

Preposition: A word or group of words that shows the relation between its object and some other word in the sentence. See Parts of Speech.

> *The murals in restaurants are on a par with the food in museums.*—Peter De Vries

Perhaps no other rule of grammar has prompted so many to say so much as the now-outdated rule prohibiting ending a sentence with a preposition.

> *The grammar has a rule absurd*
> *Which I would call an outworn myth:*
> *A preposition is a word*
> *You mustn't end a sentence with.*
> —Berton Braley

> *What this country needs is more free speech worth listening to.*—Hansell B. Duckett

Pronoun: A word that takes the place of a noun. See Parts of Speech.

Possessive pronouns represent the possessor and the thing possessed:

> The book is *mine*.

Personal pronouns are *I, you, he, she, it,* and their inflected forms (*me, my, your, them,* etc.).

Relative pronouns (who, which, that, what) join adjective clauses to their antecedents (i.e., what they refer to):

> The girl *who* sang is here.

Restrictive Elements: Words, phrases, or clauses that are essential to the meaning.

Run-on: The error in which two independent clauses are written as a single sentence, without any conjunction or punctuation separating them.

> The tennis match ended in a tie everyone agreed that it was too late to play a tie-breaker.

This error would be corrected by any of the following: adding a semicolon between the two clauses; making the clauses into separate sentences; or adding a comma and a conjunction between the clauses.

> The tennis match ended in a tie; everyone agreed that it was too late to play a tie-breaker.

> The tennis match ended in a tie. Everyone agreed that it was too late to play a tie-breaker.

> The tennis match ended in a tie, but everyone agreed that it was too late to play a tie-breaker.

Sentence: A combination of words that contains at least one subject and predicate (grammatical definition); a group of words that expresses a complete thought (popular definition).

A *simple sentence* consists of subject and predicate; in other words, an independent clause.

> *Our national flower is the concrete cloverleaf.*
> —Lewis Mumford

A *compound sentence* consists of two or more independent clauses.

> *Life is a shipwreck, but we must not forget to sing in the lifeboats.*—Voltaire

A *complex sentence* consists of one independent clause and one or more dependent (subordinate) clauses; in the following example, the independent clause is underlined.

> *New York is the only city in the world where you can be deliberately run down on the sidewalk by a pedestrian.*—Russell Baker

Subject: The part of a sentence about which something is said.

> *Time flies.*

You can identify the subject by putting *what* or *who* in front of the verb; your answer to the question thus formed is the subject.

> *Some people think they are worth a lot of money because they have it.*—Edmund Fuller

Subjective Case: Nominative case. See Case.

Subordinate Clause: See Clause, Dependent.

Suffix: A word element added to the end of a root or stem word, serving to make a new word or an inflected form of the word: gentle*ness*, mother*hood*, depend*able*, hilari*ous*, end*ed*, child*ren*, walk*ing*.

Synonym: A word having a meaning identical with or very similar to that of another word. See Antonym.

shout/yell   likely/probable

Unit Modifier: See Compound Adjective.

Verb: A word that expresses action, being, or occurrence. See Parts of Speech and Predicate.

Voice: See Active Voice, Passive Voice.

Bibliography

Bernstein, Theodore M., *The Careful Writer: A Modern Guide to English Usage,* New York: Atheneum, 1965.

Boston, Bruce O., ed., *STET! Tricks of the Trade for Writers and Editors,* Alexandria, VA: Editorial Experts, Inc., 1986.

Chicago Guide to Preparing Electronic Manuscripts, Chicago: University of Chicago Press, 1987.

Chicago Manual of Style, The, 13th ed., Chicago: University of Chicago Press, 1982.

Cook, Claire Kehrwald, *The MLA's Line by Line: How to Edit Your Own Writing,* Boston: Houghton Mifflin Co., 1985.

Copperud, Roy H., *American Usage and Style: The Consensus,* New York: Van Nostrand Reinhold, 1980.

Goodman, Michael B., *Write to the Point: Effective Communication in the Workplace,* Englewood Cliffs, NJ: Prentice-Hall, Inc., 1984.

Mitchell, Joan P., *The New Writer: Tehcniques for Writing Well with a Computer,* Redmond, WA: Microsoft Press, 1987.

Sabin, William A., *The Gregg Reference Manual,* 6th ed., New York: Gregg Division/McGraw-Hill Book Co., 1984.

Strunk, William Jr. and E.B. White, *The Elements of Style,* 3rd ed., New York: The Macmillan Co., 1979.

Success with Words: A Guide to the American Language,
Pleasantville, NY: The Reader's Digest Association, Inc., 1983.

Venolia, Jan, *Better Letters: A Handbook of Business and
Personal Correspondence,* Berkeley, CA: Ten Speed Press,
1982.

———————— *Rewrite Right! How to Revise Your Way to
Better Writing,* Berkeley, CA: Ten Speed Press, 1987.

Words into Type, 3rd ed., Englewood Cliffs, NJ:
Prentice-Hall, Inc., 1974.

Grammar Hotlines

A number of colleges in the United States and Canada operate
Grammar Hotlines. Staffed by graduate students, faculty members, and retired teachers, these hotlines will answer short
questions about writing, grammar, punctuation, spelling, dic-
tion, and syntax. For a free copy of the Grammar Hotline
Directory, send a self-addressed, stamped No. 10 envelope
(business size) to:

> Grammar Hotline Directory
> Tidewater Community College Writing Center
> 1700 College Crescent
> Virginia Beach, VA 23456

The directory is updated each January.

Frequently Misspelled Words

Note: The following list contains several pairs of "sound-alikes." A brief definition (in parentheses) identifies the first of the sound-alike words; the second sound-alike (indented) is defined at its alphabetical entry.

A

abacus
aberration
abridgment
abscess
abscissa
absence
abstinence
accelerator
accept (receive)
  except
accessible
accessory
accommodate
accumulate
achievement
acknowledgment
acquiesce
acquittal
acumen
acupuncture
adjourn
adolescence
advantageous
advertisement

aegis
aerosol
affidavit
aging
algae
algorithm
align
alimony
alkaline
allegiance
allotment
allotted
all right
already
amanuensis
amoeba
amplifier
anachronism
analogous
analysis
ancillary
anesthetic
annihilate
anomaly
anonymous
antecedent

antihistamine
apartheid
aperture
aphrodisiac
apparatus
apparel
apparent
appraisal
apropos
aqueduct
arctic
arraign
arteriosclerosis
arthritis
ascorbic
asphyxiate
aspirin
assessor
assistance
asterisk
asymmetry
attendance
attorneys
auditor
autumn
auxiliary

B

bachelor
bailiff
balance
ballistic
balloon
ballot
bankruptcy
barbecue
barbiturate
barrel
basically
beige
beneficiary
benign
bereave
berserk
bifurcate
bigot
bilateral
bilingual
binary
biodegradable
biopsy
bipartisan
blatant
bloc (group)
bludgeon
bologna
bouillon (soup)
  bullion
bourgeois
boutique
boycott
braille
brief
bruise
budget

bullion (gold)
  bouillon
bureaucracy
burglar
business
byte

C

caffeine
calendar
calorie
campaign
cannot
capillary
capitulate
capsule
captain
carafe
carat
carbohydrate
carburetor
Caribbean
carriage
catechism
category
cathode
Caucasian
caucus
caveat
ceiling
cellar
cellophane
cemetery
censor
census
centigrade
centimeter
centrifugal

cerebral
certain
cesarean
  (or Caesarean)
chaise longue
champagne
changeable
charisma
chassis
chauvinist
chiropractor
chlorophyll
chocolate
cholesterol
Christian
Cincinnati
cipher
circuit
cirrhosis
cite (quote)
  sight
  site
clone
clothes
coalition
cocaine
coefficient
cognac
coliseum
  (or colosseum)
collaborate
collar
collateral
colloquial
cologne
colonel
colossal
column
commitment

commodities
compatible
competent
computer
concurrence
condemn
conductor
conduit
conglomerate
conjugal
Connecticut
conscience
consensus
consortium
continuum
corps
correspondence
counterfeit
coup d'état
courtesy
cousin
cryptic
cul-de-sac
culinary
curtain
cybernetics
cylinder
czar

D

database
debit
debugging
decadence
deceive
decibel
deciduous

deductible
defendant
deferred
deficit
depot
depreciate
descend
desiccate
desperate
deterrent
develop
diagnostic
diaphragm
dichotomy
dictionary
diesel
digital
dilemma
dinosaur
director
disappear
disappoint
disburse (pay out)
  disperse
discernible
discreet (cautious)
discrete (separate)
disperse (scatter)
  disburse
dissatisfied
dissipate
distributor
doubt
dyeing (coloring)
dying (death)

E

eccentric
echelon

eclectic
ecstasy
effluent
eighth
either
elevator
elicit (draw forth)
  illicit
embarrass
emphysema
empirical
encyclopedia
endeavor
entrepreneur
envelope
epitome
equipped
equity
equivocal
errata
erratic
erroneous
esoteric
esthetic
  (or aesthetic)
euphemism
euthanasia
exacerbate
exaggerate
except (other than)
  accept
exhaust
exhibition
exhilarate
existential
exonerate
exorbitant
exponential
extraterrestrial

F

facsimile
factor
fallacy
familiar
faze (disturb)
  phase
feasibility
feature
February
fetus
fiduciary
fierce
filibuster
finesse
fission
flourish
fluorescent
fluoridate
foreign
foreseeable
foreword
forfeit
franchise
freight
fulfill

G

galaxy
gallon
garrulous
gauge
genealogy
generic
geriatrics
gestalt
ghetto

gourmet
governor
graffiti
grammar
grateful
grief
grievance
guarantee
guerrilla
  (or guerilla)
guess
gynecology

H

hallucinogen
harass
havoc
Hawaiian
height
heinous
heir
hemorrhage
herbicide
heroin (drug)
hertz
hiatus
hierarchy
hirsute
holistic
holocaust
hologram
homogeneous
homonym
hors d'oeuvre
hospice
hydraulic
hygiene
hymn

hypnosis
hypocrisy

I

ideology
idiosyncrasy
idle (inactive)
idol (image)
ignorance
illicit (forbidden)
  elicit
imbroglio
impeccable
impermeable
impetus
impresario
imprimatur
inadvertent
incalculable
incessant
incidentally
incumbent
independent
indictment
indispensable
inertia
infrared
innocuous
innuendo
inoculate
insecticide
intermittent
interrupt
intravenous
iridescent
irrelevant
irresistible
irrevocable

irrigate
island

J

janitor
jeopardize
jewelry
journey
judgment
junta

K

khaki
kibbutz
kilometer
kilowatt
knowledge

L

label
labyrinth
laissez faire
laser
league
legislature
leisure
leukemia
liable
liaison
libel
license
lieu
lieutenant

lightning
likable
likelihood
liquefy
liquor
logarithm
logistics
lunar

M

mahogany
maintain
maintenance
malignant
mandatory
maneuver
manila
maraschino
margarine
marijuana
marital
marshal
martial
martyr
Massachusetts
massacre
mathematics
matrix
mayonnaise
mediocre
megabyte
megawatt
memento
menstruation
metaphor
metastasize
microfiche

micrometer
microprocessor
migraine
mileage
milieu
millimeter
minestrone
miniature
minuscule
minutiae
miscellaneous
mischievous
missile
misspell
mnemonic
moccasin
modem
molecular
monetary
monitor
morass
mortgage
mustache
myopia

N

naive
narcissism
necessary
neither
neophyte
nickel
niece
noxious
nozzle
nuance
nuclear

O

obesity
occasion
occurrence
odyssey
ombudsman
omelet
omniscient
ophthalmologist
opiate
orgy
oscillator
overrun

P

panacea
paradigm
parallel
paralyze
parameter
paraphernalia
paraplegic
parliament
parochial
pasteurized
percolator
per diem
peremptory
perennial
perimeter
peripheral
permissible
perquisite
personnel
perspiration
pertinent
pharmaceutical

phase (aspect)
  faze
Philippines
phosphorus
physician
physics
pinnacle
placebo
plebiscite
pneumonia
poisonous
pollutant
polyester
polymer
porcelain
porous
Portuguese
posthumous
potpourri
prairie
precede
precious
preferred
prerogative
prevalent
privilege
procedure
proceed
programmer
propeller
prophecy (noun)
prophesy (verb)
protegé
protein
protocol
proxy
pseudonym
psychology
ptomaine

publicly
Puerto Rico

Q

quasi
questionnaire
queue
quiche
quixotic
quorum

R

radar
rapport
rarefy
rebuttal
recede
receipt
receive
receptacle
recession
reciprocal
recommend
reconnaissance
recuperate
recurrence
referred
rehearsal
relevant
religious
remembrance
remittance
renaissance
renege
rescind
resistance
restaurant

resuscitate
rhetoric
rheumatism
rhythm
robotics
roentgen
rotor

S

saboteur
saccharin (noun)
sacrilegious
salmon
satellite
savvy
scenario
schedule
scissors
secretary
seizure
separate
sergeant
siege
sieve
sight (vision)
   cite
   site
silhouette
similar
simulate
simultaneous
sinecure
sinus
siphon
site (location)
   cite
   sight
skeptical

solar
sophomore
spaghetti
stratagem
strategy
stupefy
subpena
   (or subpoena)
subterranean
subtle
succeed
succinct
suffrage
superintendent
supersede
supervisor
surprise
surveillance
syllable
synagogue
syndicate
synonymous
synopsis
syntax
syphilis

T

tariff
therapy
thief
threshold
tobacco
tongue
toxin
trafficking
tranquilizer
trauma
treasurer

trek
tyranny

U

ubiquitous
umbilical
unanimous
unerring
unnecessary
unprecedented
usage

V

vacillation
vacuum
vehicle
vengeance
verbatim
versatile
veterinarian
vice versa
vicious
vicissitude
villain
visitor

W, Y, Z

waiver
weird
wholly
withheld
womb
woolen
yacht
yield
zucchini

Index

Italicized words refer to the section entitled *Confused and Abused Words*, pp. 93–110.